# M·O·S·A·I·C ™
# QUICK TOUR
## FOR MAC

ACCESSING AND NAVIGATING THE INTERNET'S WORLD WIDE WEB

## GARETH BRANWYN

VENTANA
PRESS

**Mosaic Quick Tour for Mac: Accessing & Navigating the Internet's World Wide Web**
Copyright ©1994 by Gareth Branwyn

Branwyn, Gareth.
    Mosaic quick tour. Mac-edition : accessing and navigating the
Internet's world wide web / Gareth Branwyn. -- 1st ed.
       p.     cm.
    Includes bibliographical references and index.
    ISBN 1-56604-195-3
    1. Internet (Computer network)   2. Hypertext systems.
  I. Title.
  TK5105.875.I57B72   1994
  025.04--dc20                94-30002
                           CIP
Book design: Marcia Webb
Cover design: Spring Davis-Charles, One-of-a-Kind Design; Dawne Sherman
Cover illustration: David Watts
Index service: Mark Kmetzko
Technical advisor: Sean Carton
Technical review: Gary Moore
Editorial staff: Angela Anderson, Walter R. Bruce, III, Diana Merelman, Pam Richardson, Jessica Ryan
Production staff: Patrick Berry, Dan Koeller, Dawne Sherman, Marcia Webb
Proofreader: Eric Edstam

First Edition 9 8 7 6 5 4 3 2 1
Printed in the United States of America

Ventana Press, Inc.
P.O. Box 2468
Chapel Hill, NC 27515
919/942-0220   FAX 919/942-1140

**Limits of Liability and Disclaimer of Warranty**

95- 1209
30893181

# TRADEMARKS

Trademarked names appear throughout this book. Rather than list the names and entities that own the trademarks or insert a trademark symbol with each mention of the trademarked name, the publisher states that it is using the names only for editorial purposes and to the benefit of the trademark owner with no intention of infringing upon that trademark.

# ABOUT THE AUTHOR

Gareth Branwyn is a freelance writer and hypermedia designer. He is a regular contributor to *Wired* magazine, the senior editor of *bOING bOING* (a pop culture humor mag) and the former Street Tech editor of *Mondo 2000*. His book publishing credits include chapters in *Mondo 2000's User's Guide to the New Edge* (HarperPerennial, 1992), *Flame Wars* (Duke University Press, 1994), *Virtual Reality Casebook* (Van Nostrand Reinhold, 1994), *The Multimedia Home Companion* (Warner Books, 1995) and *The Millennial Whole Earth Catalog* (Harper San Franscisco, 1994). He is currently co-editing *bOING bOING's Happy Mutant Handbook* (Putnam Berkeley, forthcoming). As a hypermedia designer he is co-creator of the critically acclaimed *Beyond Cyberpunk!*, an electronic compendium of cyberculture. Gareth has been a flag-waving Net citizen since 1987.

# ACKNOWLEDGMENTS

First and foremost I want to thank Sean Carton. He was my right-hand man on this project and contributed ideas, material, Net wisdom and ace datasurfing talents, all beyond the call of duty. This is his book too.

The other members of my book team were my wife Pam and son Blake. They helped keep my spirits up, shoved food under my office door and kept me from yakking on the phone when I was supposed to be working.

I'd also like to thank the software developers at NCSA for making such a great piece of freeware. The authors of the freeware covered in this book are to be thanked and commended. It was a great feeling to be working on a book where almost all of the software covered is available free to anyone who has the means to download it. And it's not just free software, it's good free software.

# CONTENTS

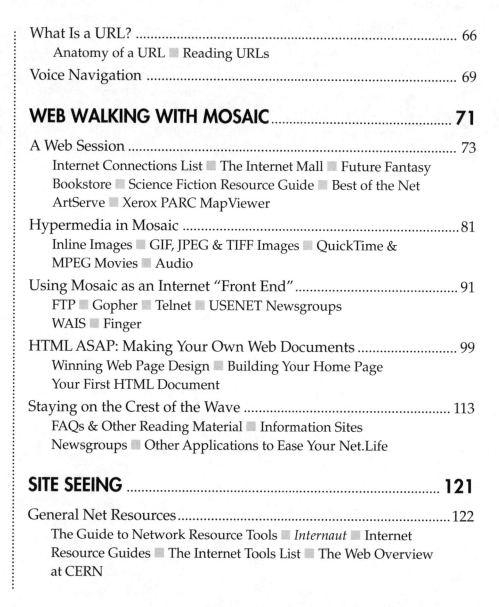

## 4  WEB WALKING WITH MOSAIC ................................... 71

## 5  SITE SEEING ........................................................ 121

# INTRODUCTION

Imagine the world's largest living document—thousands and thousands of text, graphic, audio and video files interlinked throughout the world. Well that's the World Wide Web and Mosaic is your key to that world.

The guide you hold in your hands is your entry into the world of hypermedia. Inside you'll learn Mosaic's simple graphic interface, the functions of its many menus and user-configurable features, and most importantly, how to use its navigation tools so you can effortlessly scramble through the hypermedia web that's been cast over the Internet. With Mosaic, you'll be able to view online magazines, complete with graphics, sounds and even moving images. You'll be able to ask "robot librarians" to help you search the Net for information. These automated programs will worm their way through the Net and report their findings back to you. Whether it's recreation, education, art and literature, or the latest in computer technology you're looking for, you can easily find it on the Net with Mosaic as your guide. In fact, Mosaic is not only a hypermedia information browser, you can also use it to access many standard Internet services such as Gopher, WAIS, FTP and USENET News (read only). All this makes Mosaic, and its forthcoming commercial offspring, the platform to watch as the Internet continues to make its way into the mainstream of American life.

The "catch" here is that to use Mosaic, you'll need a full-blown Internet connection. If you're not sure whether you can justify an Internet hook-up or you're unsure of what type you need, read on...

## Decisions, Decisions...

All Net connections are not created equal. They can run from cheap email-only accounts to expensive direct lines. Today, the question is not "Do I need to connect?" as much as *How* do I connect?" Choosing a method of Net access doesn't have to mean a descent into the pit of computer geekdom, weird acronyms and impenetrable jargon. However, you *will* need to decide on a few things beforehand:

- Do I need a direct, SLIP/PPP or standard dial-up connection?
- How fast a connection do I need?
- How much do I want to spend?

Internet connections are usually divided into three types:

- Direct, or "dedicated," connections (between your computer and the Internet).

  Dedicated connections are the most desirable because they give you access to all the Internet services (including things like Mosaic and Internet radio), at high speeds, 24 hours a day.

- Temporary dial-up, commonly called "SLIP/PPP," connections (your connection is routed through a local service provider).

  A more inexpensive alternative to the direct connection is the temporary dial-up, or SLIP or PPP, connection. Using a standard high-speed modem (14,400 baud) and special software, you can fool your home computer into thinking it's a big wheel on the information superhighway.

- Dial-up accounts (your computer becomes a terminal on a local host computer that's connected to the Internet).

  On a dial-up account, you phone into a Net-connected computer where you have an "account." With this type of indirect or "host" connection, all of your interactions with the Internet are through programs that run on the host machine. When you read email and USENET News, transfer files or do anything else, you can only use programs (usually text-based, icky UNIX programs) that run on the host. This type of connection is cheap and perfectly adequate if all you're looking for is the basic services like email, telnet, FTP, Gopher and newsgroups. Unfortunately, you cannot run Mosaic, Fetch, Eudora or any of the other programs mentioned in this book with this type of account.

*Note: You may even be directly connected to the Net already! If you use a locally networked computer at a large institution or corporation, you may already be wired into the Net and not even know it. Check with your systems administrator.*

## Hardware & Software Requirements

Before we begin there are some basic hardware and software requirements that must be met to be able to access the Internet through Mosaic.

- Any Macintosh computer with a hard drive.
- System 7 (or later).
- At least 4mb of RAM (8 highly recommended).
- A color Mac is needed to make use of Mosaic's color features and movies.
- A 14,400 baud modem (or faster).
- A SLIP or PPP dial-up Internet account (or a direct connection).
- MacTCP 2.0.4 software (2.0.2 will work, but 2.0.4 is recommended).

Although Mosaic will run on Macs of Classic/SE vintage (if properly souped up and network connected), in the interest of keeping caveats and disclaimers to a minimum, *Mosaic Quick Tour* assumes you're running a machine with a full-size color monitor. If you feel snubbed, we apologize. The parts of this book that don't apply to you will probably be obvious, such as discussions of color options and many of the Helper Applications, such as QuickTime. If you are on a small-screen Mac or a PowerBook, you'll want to resize the Mosaic window and turn off the Status Messages and the URL field to maximize screen size. You'll also need to make sure that Underlining Hotlinks is checked in the Preferences window so that you can see hotlinks in the Mosaic documents.

There is a special Power Macintosh version of Mosaic. It is available at the same FTP sites listed in this guide where the regular Mac versions are stored.

## How to Use *Mosaic Quick Tour*

This book was written using the Alpha 2 version of Mosaic 2.0. By the time you read this, there will probably be higher Alpha versions, or maybe even the full-blown 2.0 release. Regardless of what version of Mosaic you're using, from 1.x to 2.x, the documentation in *Mosaic Quick Tour* will be applicable. In 2.x, some of the features have been expanded (Hotlists, Preferences and Styles) and a few things have been added, such as forms support, speech recognition (usable with System 7.5) and custom menus (forthcoming). The menus have also gone through some rearrangement, but most of the features and functions they offer remain unchanged. As I write this, a number of commercial versions of Mosaic are also under development. Hopefully they will stay close enough to the current freeware versions so that what you learn in this *Quick Tour* will be directly relevant or easily translatable.

Mosaic and the World Wide Web it accesses are experiencing a period of intense growth—changes occur daily. This book and its online companion are designed to provide you with the basic knowledge and resources you need to navigate your own course through this

**Ventana Visitors Center**   To stay abreast of all late breaking news and information on Mosaic, the World Wide Web and *Mosaic Quick Tour*, why not add the Ventana Visitors Center to your hotlists menu, or better yet, make it your home page! The Visitor Centers URL is http://www.vmedia.com (see Chapter 3 for details). At the Center you can also get the latest versions of Mosaic, the default Helper Applications and many of the other excellent freeware programs mentioned in this book. If you have no idea what I'm talking about, don't worry—that's why I wrote this book.

newest wrinkle in cyberspace. Once you've made it into the main current of the data flow, you should have no trouble keeping up with the changes as they happen. It's an exciting time to be on the Net.

## Super-Duper Mosaic Quick Start

Luckily, Mosaic is fairly easy to learn and simple to use. Once you have your SLIP/PPP (or other network) connection, all you do is double-click on the Mosaic icon and you will be automatically logged into the Home Page at the National Center for Supercomputing Applications (NCSA). Welcome to Mosaic! From the Home Page, you can read the introductory information, click on *hyperlinks* (highlighted in blue) and browse through online demos and documentation (located under the "Navigate" menu and System 7's "Balloon Help" icon). When you're through being a big shot and wandering around on your own, you can either (1) proceed to the "Mosaic Quick Peek" section in Chapter 2, or (2) browse the following chapter synopsis to find out where to go next.

## What's Inside

Chapter 1, "The Net & the Web," provides a brief look at the Internet's recent growth rate and the wild and wacky metaphors that are often used to describe this exciting and ever-changing electronic world. Also covered are the circuitous history of hypermedia, the surprising emergence of the World Wide Web, a hypermedia system for the Internet and the growing popularity of Mosaic, the free "front-end" software that lets you explore the Web.

   Chapter 2, "Getting Started," gives instructions on how to get Mosaic up and running on your machine. It covers what hardware, software and network connections you need, where to find Mosaic on the Internet and how to download it, unstuff it and configure it for use. Read the "Mosaic Quick Peek" section to learn more about Mosaic's main navigation features.

Chapter 3, "Cruising Mosaic's Menus," provides a detailed tour of all the features offered in Mosaic. Includes menu items, navigating and using URLs, hyperlinks, inline images and hotlinked media, installing Helper Applications, and changing type styles.

Chapter 4, "Web Walking With Mosaic," covers how to use Mosaic to keep up with what's happening in cyberspace by taking you on a jaunt through the Web and by discussing how to use Mosaic for accessing Internet services such as FTP, telnet, newsgroup reading and Gopher; how to create your own HTML documents; how to get and use HTML editors; and how to link up with others using and discussing Mosaic.

Chapter 5, "Site Seeing," lists a directory of Web documents useful for beginners as well as sites offering libraries, look-up services and a diverse range of cool hypermedia resources available to Mosaic users.

The Appendix details the new features found in Mosaic 2.x.

A complete glossary, bibliography and index are also included.

## HOT TIP

The trick to gaining an upper hand with new software is knowing what things are called and how to look them up. If the book has a good index, and you know the terms, you can find the information you need, when you need it. *Mosaic Quick Tour* has a glossary of most of the keywords you'll encounter in Mosaic. Familiarize yourself with them and looking things up will be much easier.

So, dear friend, grab a cup of coffee (catnip tea, or whatever you drink), park yourself in your hydraulic ergonomic chair, fire up the ol' Macintosh and get ready to jack into hyperspace.

Gareth Branwyn
July 1994
gareth@vmedia.com

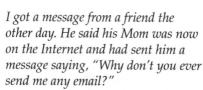

# THE NET & THE WEB

Everyone is pouring into cyberspace. Just a few years ago, friends'
and family members' eyes would glaze over whenever I would start
talking about the Internet. They'd get that "Uh oh, he's talking about
geek stuff" look on their faces and they'd start nodding politely (or
nodding off) till I was through with my little Net sermon. Now, many
of these same people have Internet addresses printed on their business
cards!

The Net has become hip, essential to modern life. Ma, Pa and the
kids want in on the action. Trolling the Net looking for news stories has
become a full-time job for journalists and TV talk-show researchers.
The business community is also hitching up its wagon trains and
heading into the vast uncharted territory of cyberspace.

Current estimates put the size of the Internet at over 2 million sites
and some 20 million users worldwide. While these figures are hotly
debated by Net statisticians, and increasing as I write this, they give
you some idea of the magnitude of this mushrooming electronic world.

Given the invisible, almost mystical nature of cyberspace, grasping for metaphors is a common pastime among Net enthusiasts. "Super-highway" and "lawless frontier" are the most frequent allusions. "Mushrooms" may be as apt as anything else. On a daily basis, networks and sites, large and small, pop up, like fungal growth in the fertile loam of ever-cheapening hardware, software and network access. This, coupled with the evangelism and hard work of thousands of Net pioneers, has led to phenomenal growth. The Internet and its constituent networks have created a global "cooperative anarchy," neither centrally located nor centrally administrated. It is growing "organically," without the benefit (or burden) of a master plan.

Another apt analogy for the Net can be drawn from Neil Stephenson's recent cyberpunk novel *Snow Crash* (1992). In Stephenson's near-future world, a floating city is being formed off the coast of California. Attracted by a mysterious cult figure, thousands of people, in ships, yachts, motor boats and anything else that floats, are attaching themselves to this huge flotilla. Decks, gangways, planked walkways and bridges connect the ever-growing mass. The Internet is much like this structure (minus the evil cult leader). People have become so attracted to the services, information mother lode and virtual community offered by the Net that they're using whatever means they can to float into it. Some come in tiny boats (SLIP/PPP connections), others on huge cruisers and fancy yachts (workstations, government and university systems). But once connected, all have at their disposal access to the electronic city, floating in the mysterious ethers of cyberspace.

While all these metaphors are limiting, and ultimately silly, they are a fun way of visualizing this new realm of technoculture, and they sometimes come in handy when explaining the life and structure of the Internet to newcomers. The reigning metaphors that frame this book and the world it explores are webs—webs as elegant, interlaced pieces of fabric, and webs as spider's lairs that ensnare all that wander into them.

As the Internet (the Net for short) has spread across the globe, users have struggled to find better ways of making more efficent use of its expanding resources. The World Wide Web, a system for linking, or weaving together, the far-flung resources of the Internet, is one recent answer to this problem. But this system simply makes data sites on the Net capable of being woven together. Something is needed to combine the disparate parts into a whole. That something is Mosaic, a program that brings a new level of information access, bandwidth and organization to the Internet. But we're getting a little ahead of ourselves. Let's take a look at some of the historical precedents that led to the emergence of the Web.

## The Curious Growth of Hypermedia

When Apple Computer released HyperCard in 1987, no one really knew what to make of it, or exactly how to use it. It was the first widely available program to create hypertext, an idea that had been floating around the computer industry and academia since Ted Nelson began promoting it in 1965.

Hypertext is a means of linking computer-based documents in associative, nonlinear ways. For example, this is how hypertext could work: you're reading a biography of Abraham Lincoln and you come to a reference to the Gettysburg Address. Simply by clicking on the words "Gettysburg Address," you can be linked to the full text of that famous speech. After reading it, you can either go back to your place in the Lincoln bio, or you can click on other links within the Gettysburg Address, wandering down an information pathway that you make up as you go along.

Early promoters of hypertext hailed it as a revolution in learning, allowing one to combine linear study with self-exploration and chance discovery. Oddly enough, HyperCard, created by Apple programming visionary Bill Atkinson, was not actually intended as a hypertext program, although that turned out to be one of its most intriguing features. Bundled free with all new Macs, HyperCard was easy to use and yet quite sophisticated. It not only had hypertext capabilities, but also offered the ability to manage and link everything from paint images to audio samples and external media devices like video disc players. Subsequent releases of HyperCard, and the other programs that followed, added the ability to link up additional graphic formats, animations and even desktop movies. This combination of hypertext and multimedia was dubbed "hypermedia." Surprisingly, people continued to struggle with the concept of hypermedia and how it could best be used. Even today, while the field of multimedia has grown, especially with the recent explosion of CD-ROM, many of the available multimedia titles make scant use of the hypertext concept. People *still* don't seem to understand what hypertext and hypermedia are all about.

It took a group of physicists from Geneva, Switzerland, to give hypermedia the big developmental boost it needed.

## The Weaving of the Web

Created at the European Particle Physics Laboratory (CERN) in Geneva, the World Wide Web (abbreviated "WWW") was originally conceived of as a Net-based hypertext exchange system that would allow European physicists to share a "universe of documents." As soon as the first implementation of the Web concept was introduced in 1991, enthusiasm quickly grew beyond the

**Is Mosaic Like Xanadu?** When introduced to Mosaic, many people ask if it is the realization of Ted Nelson's vision of Xanadu, a hypothetical worldwide hypertext system encompassing *all* written information. The answer is yes...and no. While Mosaic (and the WWW it accesses) is a hypertext/ hypermedia system that spans the globe, interlinking terabytes of information, there are differences between Mosaic and Xanadu.

- Mosaic is available free of charge, and access to many of the resources it connects to is free of charge. Xanadu is intended to be a "pay-per-view" system in which each data search is charged to you and your search results can be sold to others.
- Xanadu is not intended to be a front end for the Internet; it has one basic function. Mosaic is more than just a hypertext system; it can access most Internet services.
- Mosaic actually exists. After decades of development and hype, Xanadu is still a fantasy. →

bounds of CERN and the scientific community. Computer programmers from around the world, excited by the possibilities of "hyperlinking" documents throughout the Internet, began developing Web applications and promoting the World Wide Web online. Early users also realized that not only hypertext, but full-blown hypermedia, could be passed over the Internet using Web technology.

It now looks as though hypermedia is finally going to make an impact, but in a way that its pioneers never would have expected.

- Xanadu would be a stand-alone system. Mosaic takes advantage of the already-existing infrastructure of the Internet.
- Xanadu would be centrally administrated by a commercial entity. Mosaic is essentially decentralized and free of any one entity's control.

For more information on Xanadu, check out: http://www.aus.xanadu.com/

## Mosaic: Free & Easy

Soon after the introduction of the World Wide Web, software designers at the National Center for Supercomputing Applications (NCSA) at the University of Illinois, Urbana-Champaign, began work on a simple and powerful graphical interface for WWW. With many similarities to HyperCard, Mosaic was designed to be an easy-to-use, easy-to-build hypermedia system operated via pop-up windows, pull-down menus and "point-and-click" navigation. Except here, rather than weaving your way through the media available on a single disk drive, you weave your way through the vast resources of the Internet! Mosaic's first release in June 1993 (for X Windows) was met with great enthusiasm. Versions for Macintosh and PC soon followed. Perhaps more than any other piece of WWW software, Mosaic has helped fuel an explosion of interest in the World Wide Web and the possibilities of building a true "hypermedia universe" in cyberspace.

# Why Is NCSA's Mosaic So Great?

It's free! NCSA is a federally funded institution, one of four National Science Foundation supercomputing centers. One of NCSA's missions is to provide noncommercial software that can benefit the scientific community. In accomplishing this goal, NCSA has made Mosaic readily available on the Internet, to the benefit of all. In addition to its free status, Mosaic

- Runs over a SLIP/PPP connection.

- Is easy to install and intuitive to use.

- Features a simple interface using common windows/menu format and mouse-driven navigation.

- Offers online help and email technical support.

- Allows you to change type styles, size, format (bold, italic) and colors on the documents you're browsing.

- Supports audio, movies (MPEG and QuickTime), graphics (GIF, JPEG, TIFF) and binary file conversion (BinHex).

- Offers a "History" feature that lets you retrace your steps.

- Provides access to network services such as USENET News (read only), FTP, Gopher and Telnet.

- Allows you to create and store lists of frequently used documents.

- Includes a personal "Annotations" feature that lets you add written and audio notes to any Mosaic document (for your eyes only).

- Includes a "Search" feature that allows you to search through indices within documents.

- The host computer (the server) is ready to respond to your request. This scheme cuts down on Net traffic.
- Fully supports HTTP (HyperText Transport Protocol) and HTML (HyperText Markup Language), the current standards for WWW communication and presentation of information.

## What in Cyberspace Is HTML?

HTML, or HyperText Markup Language, is the language the World Wide Web speaks. Web documents written in HTML contain formatting codes that tell Web browsing software (such as Mosaic) how to present the various components of a document to the user. HTML is so simple to use that many Web users have become Web producers. Similar to the rapid proliferation and exchange of HyperCard stacks, generated soon after that program's release, HTML has fostered a boon in creating WWW documents. The beauty of webbed hypermedia is that, once Web-accessible, it can be hyperlinked to other sites, building, organically, that vast universe of hypermedia now under construction.

## What Does the Future Hold?

Without sounding too grandiose, it is possible that Mosaic and its progeny could quickly become the standard front end for the Internet. Even though Internet "membership" is growing rapidly, many users have great difficulty figuring out how to use all the available services. This, coupled with the infoglut of too much information and no way of burrowing through it, means that the Internet experience can quickly become overwhelming. Mosaic brings the resources of the Internet back into the familiar realm of the Mac and Windows graphic user environments. Few average users know what an IP address is, or how to write a UNIX script; but almost everyone knows how to point and click a mouse.

For many Internet service developers, Mosaic is a major break-through. Government agencies, universities, mail-order businesses and publishers (to name a few) are all scrambling to offer their resources through Mosaic. Mitch Kapor, founder of the Electronic Frontier Foundation (EFF) and a chief evangelist for the information highway, sees Mosaic as a major turning point in providing free and open access.

Another likely area of development for Mosaic may be as a full-blown Internet publisher. Numerous magazines have been exploring better ways of making the leap into cyberspace, and Mosaic might be the ticket. As the software improves and modem speeds increase, full-page layouts with color graphics, animations, film clips, automated product ordering and many other features will become commonplace. Using Mosaic for video-on-demand and set-top-box interactive television is also a likely possibility.

Given the "cooperative anarchy" under which Mosaic has thus far been built and distributed, we should also expect the unexpected when thinking about its future.

## Let Me Get This Straight

If you're having trouble figuring all this out, let's recap.

**The Internet**   The global "network of networks" is currently comprised of approximately 2 million computer sites and some 20 million users. The Net is the physical hardware of computers, gateways, bridges, telephone connections and the software that runs everything.

**The World Wide Web**   The World Wide Web is a hypermedia exchange system that allows users to exchange linked text, images and sounds over the Internet. Abbreviated "WWW."

**Hypertext & Hypermedia**   Hypertext is a means of linking information in a document to allow the reader to explore non-linear connections to other documents (or parts of the same document). Hypermedia is the same concept, expanded to include graphics, moving images and sounds.

**HTML**   HyperText Markup Language (or HTML) is simply the language that all World Wide Web documents "speak."

**Mosaic**   A program that allows you to explore the resources available via the World Wide Web is called a *browser*. Mosaic is a popular WWW browser that uses a mouse-driven graphic interface to make Web navigating easy.

## Moving On

The Internet is big. We've all been witness to its amazing growth and its overshadowing hype in the media. Hype abounds...and now that hype has been turned toward the World Wide Web and Mosaic. Is this latest development as cool as people say it is? Let's look beyond the hype to some of the numbers. According to *Entering the World Wide Web*, an electronic document created by Kevin Hughes, Web growth has been phenomenal. He reports that a software "robot" was sent through the Web in June of 1993 to count all the sites offering WWW documents. This robot logged around 100 sites. In May of 1994, a similar automated traveler wove its way through 3,800 Web sites. Hughes goes on to report that the folks at NCSA, maker of Mosaic and maintainers of one of the busiest Web sites in the world, claim that they get at least 1 million connections to their site *per week*...and the number is increasing swiftly. Just one year ago, that number was 100,000 connections per week. Given this level of activity, it's clear that Mosaic and WWW *are* all the rage in cyberspace. This book gives you the information and skills you need to access the Web yourself so you can see what all the fuss is about.

So, your interest has been piqued and you're caught up on some Net and Web history; now it's time to get busy. The following chapter covers all the basics on how to find Mosaic on the Net, how to set it up on your computer and how to take your first trip through the Web. My job will be to make all this sound easy. Wish us both luck.

# GETTING STARTED

*A journey of a thousand miles begins with a full tank of gas.*
*— Anonymous*

Our trip is going to be a short one, so let's get down to business. This tour guide is not for Net novices. I'm assuming you are already familiar with the Macintosh, modems, basic telecommunications and the Internet. If you are unfamiliar with the Internet, I recommend you read Michael Fraase's *Mac Internet Tour Guide* (Ventana Press), or some other introductory book. (See the bibliography for more suggestions.) If you already have some form of File Transfer Protocol (FTP) access (such as a dial-up account), you can download electronic versions of Brendan P. Kehoe's *Zen and the Art of the Internet* from ftp.cs.widener.edu or *The Hitchhiker's Guide to the Internet* from ftp.eff.org. Search the EFF site for numerous other Net-related documents.

In this chapter you'll be given the information you need to find and download Mosaic using conventional FTP on a dial-up account and how to download it using the program Fetch over a SLIP/PPP account. After you've wrangled the program onto your hard drive and unpacked it, I'll show you how to do a basic configuration of it so that you can jump into the Web immediately to have a quick look around.

## Necessary Connections

If you are already on the Net and have Mosaic downloaded but still need to install it, skip this section and move on to "Unpacking Your Booty" on page 18. To run Mosaic, you need either a direct (or "dedicated") Internet connection (found in many businesses, government offices and universities), or you need what's called a SLIP (Serial Line Internet Protocol) or PPP (Point-to-Point Protocol) account. Many local Internet service providers now offer SLIP/PPP connections at very reasonable rates. In some cases, the cost of the SLIP/PPP connection is not a lot more than a standard dial-up connection. As these types of connections become more common, thanks in part to the growing popularity of Mosaic, service providers are making SLIP/PPP connections easier to get and to set up. Call your local provider for more information.

For an updated electronic list of Internet service providers, Peter Kaminski's PDIAL list is highly recommended. To get a current copy of the list, send the email message Send PDIAL to info-deli-server@netcom.com. If you do not yet have Net access, and therefore cannot get this list, have a wired friend download it for you.

## HOT TIP

It is a commonly held belief that SLIP/PPP connections are expensive and that the software is difficult to configure. This may have *been* the case, but the recent increased interest among Internet users for this type of connection has led to the widespread availability of MacTCP and SLIP/PPP software. Several popular book/software packages such as *The Mac Internet Tour Guide* (Ventana Press) and the *Internet Membership Kit* (Ventana Media) provide all the software you need. Many Internet providers have developed helpful scripts and installation instructions, and will walk you through the connection procedure over the phone if necessary. Several providers will even configure the software for you. Call around and find a provider that can give you the level of assistance you need. Don't be scared away from this type of connectivity. It's easier than you think.

## Downloading Mosaic

Once you have your Internet connection taken care of, you're ready to download and install Mosaic.

### Using Fetch

If you have the FTP program Fetch installed, follow these instructions:

1. Double-click on the Fetch icon to launch the program. The Open Connection dialog box will appear. See Figure 2-1.

2. Enter NCSA's FTP site address in the Host box. The address is ftp.ncsa.uiuc.edu.

3. Type **anonymous** in the User ID box.

4. Instead of a password, type in your full Net email address (username@site.domain). This is a common network convention used with anonymous logins.

5. When you click on the OK button, the Fetch animated dog icon will start moving. The little pooch will run furiously until a connection is established.

*Note: If you have trouble connecting to the NCSA site, see the list of other FTP sites that offer Mosaic in Table 2-2.*

6. Once connected, you'll see the File Browser dialog box. The left-hand window shows you the first level of the directory on the host computer

---

**Open Connection...**

Enter host name, user name, and password (or choose from the shortcut menu):

Host: `ftp.ncsa.uiuc.edu`

User ID: `anonymous`

Password:

Directory:

Shortcuts: ▼ [ Cancel ] [ OK ]

Figure 2-1: *Fetch's Open Connection dialog box.*

Figure 2-2: *Animated dog icon.*

(called the *root* directory). Scroll through this directory and navigate the folder hierarchy just as you would on your hard drive. You are looking for the Mac folder, and within that folder, the Mosaic folder.

7. Once inside Mosaic, you should see a file called NCSAMosaicMac.200A2.sea.hqx, or whatever the latest version is labeled (see Figure 2-3).

8. Click on the Get File... button and the file transfer will begin. (Look at that little pooch go!) When completed, click on the Close Connection button (or hit Command+W) and you'll be disconnected from the FTP server.

9. If you have Automatic File Opening active, the file will be automatically unpacked.

10. Congratulations. You are now the proud owner of Mosaic.

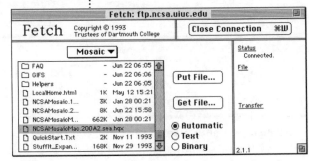

Figure 2-3: *The File Browser dialog box showing the Mosaic files at NCSA.*

| Site Name | Directory Path |
| --- | --- |
| bitsy.mit.edu | /pub/mac |
| mac.archive.umich.edu | /mac/util/comm |

Table 2-1: *If you don't already have Fetch, you can get it, using conventional FTP, from these two sites.*

## Using Traditional FTP on a Dial-up Account

### 3W: The Internet With a Human Face

Magazines devoted to the Internet and computer communications used to be boring—technical, academic, drab—boring. A magazine from England called *3W: Global Networking News-letter* has changed all that. Created by a group called Art + Computers, *3W* looks like a stylish print magazine that just happens to be about the Internet. *3W* avoids technical jargon, is geared toward all levels of users and doesn't talk down to new Net citizens. It takes an artful approach to computers while still managing to fill its pages with useful information. The magazine's motto, "The Internet with a Human Face," expresses its interest in the people part of the Internet equation rather than the technology. *3W* fosters a sense of "virtual community" on the Internet. Each issue includes listings of new sites, Net happenings and significant personalities. There are also articles on regional networks, BBSes and Internet administration. A WWW column contains descriptions and URLs of notable Web sites. If you want to stay plugged in (and still have a special place in your heart for high-quality print magazines), you may want to check out *3W*. For the latest subscription information, send email to 3W@ukartnet.demon.co.uk, or check their Web page at http://www.3W.com/3W/

1. Log into your account as you normally would.

2. At the prompt, type **ftp ftp.ncsa.uiuc.edu** (The double ftp is not a mistake: the first ftp is the command; the second is part of the address of the FTP site.)

3. Press Return and you will soon be connected to the NCSA FTP server.

4. At the login prompt, type **anonymous**. When asked for a password, type in your full Internet email address (username@site.domain). This is a common network convention used with anonymous logins.

*Note: If you have trouble connecting to the NCSA site, see the list of other FTP "mirror" sites in Table 2-2.*

5. Once inside the FTP server, you want to type the directory path you'll need to get to the Mosaic files. That path is Mac/Mosaic

6. From inside the Mosaic file area, type **ls** and press Return. That's the UNIX command for a directory list. Among the items listed, you should see NCSAMacMosaic.200A2.sea.hqx (or whatever the latest version is called).

7. The .hqx at the end of the file name indicates that the file has been compressed with BinHex and stored as a text file. You will need to tell the host computer you want it downloaded as a text file by typing **ascii**. It should respond with "Type set to A."

8. To retrieve the program, type **get NCSAMacMosaic.200A2.sea.hqx** (or whatever the file is currently called). The file will then be transferred.

*Note: If you are on a dial-up connection, the file will be downloaded to your local host computer. Consult the manual provided with your dial-up Internet account (and your modem software manual) if you are unfamiliar with how to get the file from their machine to yours.*

Due to the popularity of Mosaic, the NCSA sites handle huge amounts of traffic. To ease this traffic jam, try downloading Mosaic from one of the additional FTP sites found in Table 2-2 below.

| Site Name | Directory Path |
|---|---|
| ftp.vmedia.com | /pub/companions/mosaicqt/mac/mosaic |
| sunsite.unc.edu | /pub/packages/infosystems/WWW/clients/Mosaic/Mosaic-Mac/ |
| journal.biology.carleton.ca | /pub/mirrors/ftp.ncsa.uiuc.edu/Mac/Mosaic |
| miriworld.its.unimelb.edu.au | /pub/clients/Macmosaic |
| ftp.luth.se | /pub/infosystems/www/ncsa/Mac |
| ftp.sunet.se | /pub/mac/Mosaic |

Table 2-2: *Other FTP sites offering Mosaic.*

Mosaic has been widely distributed throughout the Internet. Besides the FTP sites above, many online services and other "islands in the Net" have it in their software libraries. Look around and download using whatever method you are most comfortable with.

- Check America Online, CompuServe or other services you may have access to.

  - The Ventana Visitors Center, which can be accessed as follows:

    | | |
    |---|---|
    | Gopher | gopher.vmedia.com |
    | FTP | ftp.vmedia.com |
    | WWW | http://www.vmedia.com/ |
    | email | info@vmedia.com |

    In body of message type **send help** (This will send more info about the center, *not* the Mosaic program itself.)

  - Art and Farces

    | | |
    |---|---|
    | Gopher | gopher.farces.com |
    | FTP | ftp.farces.com |
    | WWW | http://www.farces.com/ |
    | email | almanac@farces.com |

    In body of message type **send help** (This will send more info about the site, *not* the Mosaic program itself.)

  - Snail mailed from NCSA

The National Center for Supercomputing Applications, creator and maintainer of Mosaic, has a catalog of software offerings, manuals and other information. You can get a copy via email or snail mail:

| | |
|---|---|
| email | orders@ncsa.uiuc.edu |
| snail mail | NCSA Orders |
| | 152 Computing Applications Bldg. |
| | 605 East Springfield Ave. |
| | Champaign, IL 61820-5518 |

---

**The Ventana Visitors Center**  Ventana offers an Online Companion for the *Mosaic Quick Tour* as part of the Ventana Visitors Center. The Online Companion offers all the software mentioned in the *Quick Tour*, with the latest versions accessible as soon as they are made available, along with version change notes. There is also an online guide that will provide you with quick access to Internet resources related to this book. The Mosaic Quick Tour Online Companion will help make this book dynamic, up-to-date and continually useful.

The Ventana Visitor's Center can be found at **http://www.vmedia.com/vvc/index.html**

The Mosaic Quick Tour Online Companion can be found at **http://www.vmedia.com/vvc/onlcomp/mosaicqtm/index.html**

## Unpacking Your Booty

If you've downloaded Mosaic using conventional FTP through a UNIX account, you will now need to unpack it. To accomplish this, you'll need StuffIt Expander and BinHex 4.0. StuffIt Expander is widely available and comes bundled with many online services' software packages (such as AOL) and Internet access disks (*The Mac Internet Tour Guide Companion Disk,* for example). Check to see if you already have this program. If you don't, here's how to download it:

Before you can use StuffIt Expander, you need a program called BinHex 4.0 to unstuff StuffIt. Sheesh! To get BinHex 4.0, FTP to one of the sites listed in Table 2-2.

Once connected and logged in,

1. Type **cd /info-mac/cmp** and press Return.

2. Do a ls to get a file listing. Find binhex4.bin.

3. Type **bin** at the prompt (this sets the file type to binary).

4. Once the file type has been set, type **get binhex4.bin.**

   *Note: If you are using Fetch to get this program, you don't have to worry about setting the file type.*

Once you have BinHex 4.0 on your computer (see Figure 2-4), you can download StuffIt Expander from the same site. Make sure to switch the file type, by typing **ascii** at the prompt, before you download StuffIt Expander. Once you have StuffIt Expander in its .hqx format, you need to un-BinHex it.

BinHex 4.0

Figure 2-4: *BinHex 4.0 icon.*

## Un-BinHexing

To unpack StuffIt,

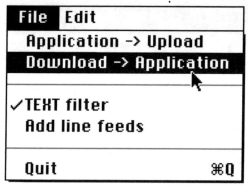

Figure 2-5: *The BinHex 4.0 File menu.*

1. Double-click on BinHex to open it. Click on the introduction screen to dismiss it.

2. Go to the File menu and select Download->Application (see Figure 2-5). This will cause a dialog box to pop up asking you what you want to un-BinHex.

3. Select your BinHexed StuffIt file and hit Open.

4. BinHex will now ask you where you want to save Stuffit Expander.sea. Select your desktop. Since StuffIt is a "drag-and-drop" application, it's handier to keep it on the desktop in plain view.

5. Select Save. When it's done un-BinHexing, choose Quit from the File menu.

## Installing StuffIt Expander

StuffIt Expander comes as a .sea file, meaning it is a "Self-Extracting Archive."

1. To install, all you have to do is double-click on the StuffIt Expander™.sea icon. A dialog box will appear.

2. Hit Continue. A dialog box will prompt "Install the Software as:" Leave the name alone and install StuffIt Expander on your desktop.

3. Hit Save. A progress bar will pop up as StuffIt Expander is being unpacked. When it's done, a dialog box saying "Installation Successful" will appear.

4. Select Quit.

You are done installing StuffIt Expander. You should now have a folder on your desktop called Stuffit Expander™. In this folder is the icon for StuffIt Expander (see Figure 2-6) and a file named "StuffIt Expander 3.0.7 Docs." Read this for more information on this invaluable utility program.

## Installing Mosaic

Relax! The hard part is over. Installing Mosaic is a piece of cake once you have StuffIt Expander ready for action.

1. To install Mosaic (once you've downloaded it) simply drag the Mosaic.hqx (or it may appear as an .sea or .sit) file over to the StuffIt Expander icon and let it go. StuffIt Expander will churn away till your file is unstuffed. You should now have a folder called NCSAMosaicMac.200A2 on your desktop. This is Mosaic!

2. Move the folder to its permanent parking spot on your hard drive. There you have it, you're done!

## Mosaic Quick Peek

To open Mosaic, regardless of what type of connection you have (SLIP/PPP or a dedicated line), you do not need to do anything before launching Mosaic. Any necessary connections will be opened for you.

Double-click on the Mosaic icon (see Figure 2-7). If everything is properly set up, the program will launch, make its network connections and then automatically connect you to the NCSA Home Page. You are now on the Web! Why not have a brief look around?

**StuffIt Expander™**

Figure 2-6: *StuffIt Expander icon. To use, simply drag stuffed files over the StuffIt Expander icon and let go.*

**NCSAMosaicMac.200A2**

Figure 2-7: *Mosaic, your doorway to the Web.*

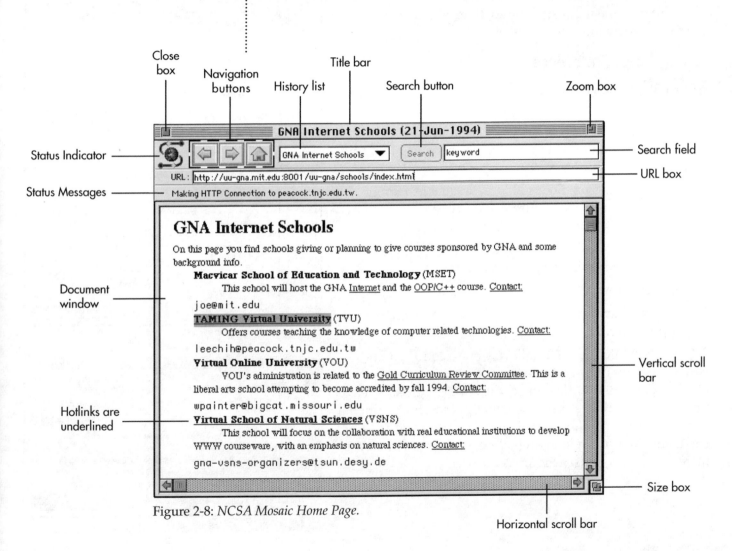

Figure 2-8: *NCSA Mosaic Home Page.*

Labels (clockwise from top):
- Close box
- Navigation buttons
- History list
- Title bar
- Search button
- Zoom box
- Search field
- URL box
- Vertical scroll bar
- Size box
- Horizontal scroll bar
- Hotlinks are underlined
- Document window
- Status Messages
- Status Indicator

Window content:

**GNA Internet Schools (21-Jun-1994)**

GNA Internet Schools ▼    Search    keyword

URL : http://uu-gna.mit.edu:8001/uu-gna/schools/index.html

Making HTTP Connection to peacock.tnjc.edu.tw.

# GNA Internet Schools

On this page you find schools giving or planning to give courses sponsored by GNA and some background info.

**Macvicar School of Education and Technology** (MSET)
    This school will host the GNA Internet and the OOP/C++ course. Contact:

joe@mit.edu

**TAMING Virtual University** (TVU)
    Offers courses teaching the knowledge of computer related technologies. Contact:

leechih@peacock.tnjc.edu.tw

**Virtual Online University** (VOU)
    VOU's administration is related to the Gold Curriculum Review Committee. This is a liberal arts school attempting to become accredited by fall 1994. Contact:

wpainter@bigcat.missouri.edu

**Virtual School of Natural Sciences** (VSNS)
    This school will focus on the collaboration with real educational institutions to develop WWW courseware, with an emphasis on natural sciences. Contact:

gna-vsns-organizers@tsun.desy.de

It's important to recall that the Net is a potential space, and Mosaic is your connection to this space. Before you go any further, in the interest of a smoother ride, there are a few things you should take care of.

## Setting Basic Preferences

1. Open the Preferences dialog box by selecting Preferences from the Options menu. See Figure 2-9.

2. Along the left-hand side, you will see four icons: Misc, Links, Dirs and Gates. Our first stop on this quick tour will be at the Misc icon.

3. Select the Misc icon. Four fields are available: Home Page, User Name, EMail Address and Background Color. For now, leave the Home Page box as it is. See Figure 2-10.

4. In the User Name box, enter your name in real life (you remember your real life name, don't you?).

5. In the EMail Address box, enter your email address.

6. When you have set everything the way you want it, click the Apply button.

7. Click the Links icon. This allows you to configure the various aspects of how Mosaic handles *hotlinks* (links to other documents). At this point, you should probably leave things the way they are, but note that in Mosaic documents *Explored links* (defaulted as red) are links you have already tried, and *Unexplored links* (defaulted as blue) are links you have yet to click on (see Figure 2-11).

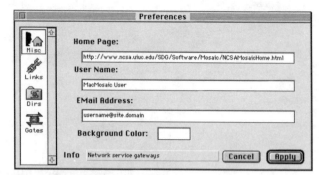

Figure 2-9: *Preferences dialog box.*

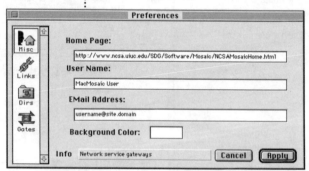

Figure 2-10: *Misc Preferences dialog box.*

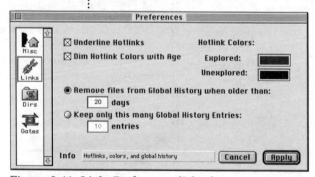

Figure 2-11: *Links Preferences dialog box.*

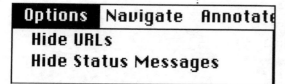

Figure 2-12: *Dirs Preferences dialog box.*

8. Click on the Dirs icon. This is where you tell Mosaic where to put files you download and where your Helper Applications are located (more on Helper Applications in Chapter 3). See Figure 2-12.

9. The Temp Directory button allows you to select the directory on your hard drive where Mosaic should put temporary files. This is defaulted to your System Folder. If you want to change this location, click on the Set Temp Directory button and select the directory where you want Mosaic to temporarily store downloaded files.

That is all the configuring you need to do in Preferences to get started in Mosaic. Here are a few more suggested configurations that are helpful for a first-time Mosaic user.

## Using URLs

1. The URL box lets you see the "address" of your current document location. In Mosaic 2.x you can also type a new URL into this box and press Return to connect with a new location. Make sure that the Show URLs feature is enabled. Select this in the Option menu. Once selected, the menu choice will read Hide URLs (see Figure 2-13). When the Show URLs is turned on, the URL box will be visible on the Mosaic Navigation Panel (see Figure 2-14).

| Options | Navigate | Annotate |
|---|---|---|
| **Hide URLs** | | |
| **Hide Status Messages** | | |

Figure 2-13: *The Show/Hide URL option.*

URL: http://www.ncsa.uiuc.edu/SDG/Software/Mosaic/NCSAMosaicHome.html

Figure 2-14: *The URL box is visible on the Navigation Panel when it's turned on.*

Note: URLs (or Uniform Resource Locators) are really the heart of Mosaic. They are discussed in much greater detail in Chapter 3.

2. Similarly, the Show Status Messages option allows you to monitor Mosaic's actions. To enable this function, make sure the words Hide Status Messages are listed in the Options menu (see Figure 2-15).

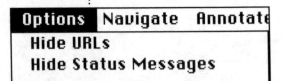

Figure 2-15: *Show Status or Hide Status is turned on and off in the Option menu.*

3. Finally, Mosaic usually installs with the Auto-Load Images feature selected. This means that when Mosaic encounters an inline image (a graphic within a Mosaic document), it will automatically display it. If you are using Mosaic over a SLIP/PPP connection, you probably want to turn this option off by selecting it from the Options menu and making sure there isn't a checkmark next to it. Otherwise, you may have to go out and run around the block a few times or take a nap every time you connect to a site with large and frequent inline images. You will still be able to view anything that interests you by clicking on the Inline Image icon.

Figure 2-16: *Inline Image icon.*

 **HOT TIP** —  · — · — · — · — · — · — · — · — · — · — · — ·—

If your Mac is on a dedicated network connection, such as a campus or corporate LAN, you can leave the Auto-Load Image feature on. Because you have a much higher transfer rate, the images shouldn't take that long to load.

— · — · — · — · — · — · — · — · — · — · — · — · — ·—

## Having a Look Around

Now...finally...you are ready to give Mosaic a whirl. The Mosaic Home Page offers plenty to keep you busy. Try clicking on some of the hotlinks. Wander, explore, have some fun.

Figure 2-17: *The Main Navigation icons.*

When you've had your fill and want to get back to the Home Page, click on the Home icon or use the Back and Forward arrow icons. The Forward arrow only works if you've moved back a document (or more) and then want to go forward again. The Back arrow takes you to the previous document. See Figure 2-17.

Haven't had enough? Look under the navigate menu for some other places to explore. And if you need some roadside assistance, check out System 7's Balloon Help icon.

## Moving On

Now that you've learned a little bit about Mosaic and have spent some time in Webspace, you've probably caught a glimpse of why everyone seems so excited. Mosaic adds a whole new level of ease and flexibility to navigating cyberspace...and God knows, today's cyberspace needs that.

The next chapter is intended to move, step-by-step, through Mosaic's basic features. Again, you probably don't have to read it all (although you know what Mom would say!). If you're feeling brave and want to learn as you go, you can jump back into Webspace with this guide in hand and then look things up when you get stuck.

**Roadside America in the Web!** The authors of the Roadside America series of wacky travel guides (most recently *New Roadside America*, Simon & Schuster 1992), hit the road again, this time taking the Internet with them. *Hypertour '94* authors Mike Wilkins, Doug Kirby and Ken Smith logged some 4,000 miles in seven days, between June 29 and July 5, 1994. They let the Internet follow their exploits by uploading daily reports and images to *Wired* magazine's Web site and to the Wired forum on America Online. They dispatched daily travel logs, photos and even QuickTime movies of their trip, stuffing all this data through the phone lines of their hotel rooms each night. Always true to their bizarre and playful curiosities, they stopped at such places as Beaver, Oklahoma, the "Cow Chip Throwing Capital of the World"; the pint-sized Stonehenge replica in Rolla, Missouri; Philippi, West Virginia, home of the West Virginia Mummies; New Vrindeban, a Krishna palace and theme park (also in West Virginia); and the creepy Mutter Museum of preserved medical oddities in Philadelphia (where the thorax of John Wilkes Booth is preserved). →

Internetters were also able to send messages to the group and get personal responses by posting messages on America Online. The trio of authors have became America's foremost authorities on out-of-the-way and unusual tourist attractions, having traveled some 100,000 miles over the years in search of the unique, the forgotten and the strange.

The archives of *Hypertour '94* are located at http://www.wired.com and in the Wired forum on America Online (keyword: wired).

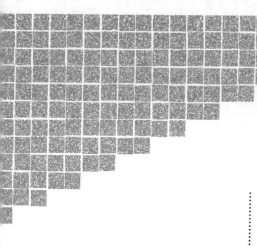

# CRUISING MOSAIC'S MENUS

*Never worry about theory as long as the machinery does what it's supposed to do.*
— *R.A. Heinlein*

**M**osaic is not a difficult program to learn. Part of its popularity is due to its familiar graphic interface and its intuitive workings. While the basics of Mosaic are easily mastered, even its more technical and esoteric aspects are approachable by most Net citizens.

This chapter covers each feature of Mosaic and gives a brief introduction to all of its menus and each item found within those menus. Before we begin our menu tour, to ensure a smooth ride through Mosaic, be sure to finish configuring your preferences (see "Setting Basic Preferences" on pages 22-23).

When our tour of Mosaic's menus is complete you'll want to

- Check to make sure that you have all the Helper Applications you'll need to view graphics and movies and to hear audio clips (see page 46).

- Learn enough about how Tag Styles work in Mosaic so that you can control the look of your Web documents (see page 52).
- Make sure that you know how the Hotlists feature works (see page 59).

## Mosaic's Menus

Let's take a trip through Mosaic's menus to see how everything works. After you've had a brief look around, you can decide where you want to go back and spend more time.

### The File Menu

If you are familiar with the Macintosh graphic user interface, you already know many functions found under the Mosaic File menu.

### New Window

Lets you open a second copy of the home page, while keeping the previous window(s) intact.

### Clone Window

Opens a copy of the current window.

### The Open URL...

One of the main tools used for moving from one Web page to another. After selecting this feature, a window appears (see Figure 3-2) with a box for entering a Uniform Resource Locator (URL). URLs are the addresses for documents accessible through the World Wide Web. You can either type in the URL or cut and paste it from another

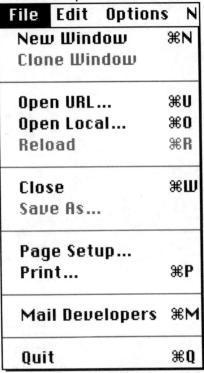

Figure 3-1: *Mosaic's File menu.*

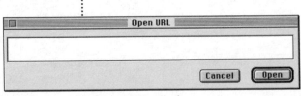

Figure 3-2: *The Open URL window.*

source. Hitting Open begins the connection to the site where that document is located. In Mosaic 2.x, the previously entered URL stays in the URL box until you type in a new one (or quit the current session). For more information on URLs, see "What Is a URL?" later in this chapter.

## Open Local

Allows you to open a local (on your hard drive) Hypertext Markup Language (HTML) or text document. Open Local is also useful for testing your homemade Web documents before you unleash them on the rest of the world.

## Reload

Causes the current Web page to be redrawn. This is useful if the document doesn't display properly, or if you're editing an HTML document and want to see the results of your changes. Reload is also used when you make changes in, or delete, an annotation and you want the changes to take effect immediately.

## Close

Closes the current Mosaic window. If you have multiple open windows or clones, it will close only the top window.

## Save As...

Allows you to save the current Mosaic document in either plain text or HTML formats. If you save a document as plain text, all HTML information will be stripped from it. This is similar to word processed documents formatted as ASCII text. All graphic elements, type stylings (bold, underline), etc., will be removed. Saving a document as HTML writes it to your hard drive as an HTML document with all *hotlinks* (links to other documents), *tags* (the actual HTML codes), *URLs* and other formatting information intact. This information is the "source code" of HTML.

## Page Setup...

Presents the standard Macintosh Page Setup dialog box.

## Print

Presents print options in the standard Print dialog box. Prints the full contents of the current document (including inline graphics and material above and/or below the Mosaic document window).

## Mail Developers

Allows you to send an email message to the software developers at NCSA. When chosen from the File menu, a window pops up with the email address of NCSA hardwired in (see Figure 3-3). All you have to do is enter the subject of your message in the appropriate box and the text of your message in the scrolling text box. When you're done, hit Send, and your pithy prose will be posted to NCSA.

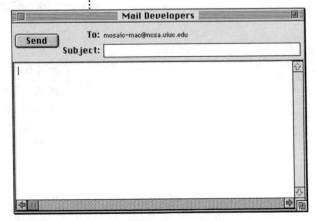

Figure 3-3: *The Mail Developers window.*

Two important things to remember:

1. Before you can send this email message, you must enter your return email address in the EMail box located in the Preferences area (under the Misc section).

2. Since Mosaic does not support other forms of email besides this outgoing message to the developers, you need to have a regular Internet address to receive an answer.

As you might imagine, the developers at NCSA get a lot of mail from Mosaic users. Please don't take advantage of this service. Before you send your question(s), make sure you've looked through *Mosaic Quick Tour*, the online Mosaic help documents (located under the Balloon Help icon) and the various Mosaic and WWW FAQ (Frequently Asked Questions) files.

When you do send a message to the Mac Mosaic developers, your message to them automatically includes your name (whatever you've entered in the User Name box in the Preferences window), the type of Mac you're using, which system software you're running and a list of all installed control panels and extensions. NCSA swears that's all the information that's nabbed from your computer...no really :-)

*Note: It's a shame that the NCSA address cannot be changed in this window. If it could, then this feature could be used as an outgoing mail box to anyone on the Net. If you'd like to be able to send and receive email during your Mosaic sessions, you can use programs such as Eudora. See Chapter 4 for more information.*

## Quit

Now I don't have to tell you what that does, do I?

### ⟲ HOT TIP

When launching Mosaic over a SLIP or PPP connection, some SLIP/PPP programs will automatically open the outgoing connection (i.e., you don't have to establish the connection before opening Mosaic). But when you quit Mosaic, they don't automatically disconnect. This can be a problem; you can stay connected for hours before noticing. Some services automatically break your connection if it remains idle for a certain amount of time. Others don't. Regardless, the best thing to do is to keep your SLIP or PPP connection window visible and to check it after leaving Mosaic.

# The Edit Menu

The Edit menu choices in Mosaic will be familiar if you've used other Mac programs. This is where you can interact with the text within Mosaic, cutting, copying, pasting, text searching and so forth.

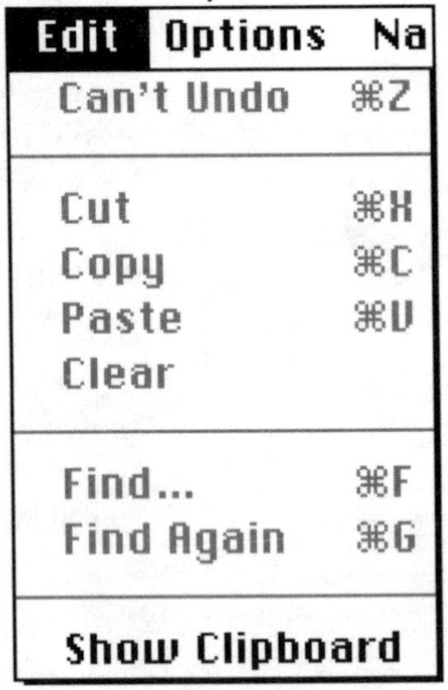

## Can't Undo

Undoes text changes, if this menu choice is highlighted; if dimmed you can't. Only works in dialog boxes and pop-up windows such as Open URL...

## Cut

Cuts (deletes) text and pastes it into the clipboard. You cannot cut text in an actual Web document, only in dialog boxes and pop-up windows.

## Copy

Copies selected text. You can copy text from a Web document, but you cannot paste text into a Web document. Copying is especially useful for grabbing text you want to paste into your personal Annotations or into a word processor.

Figure 3-4: *Mosaic's Edit menu.*

## Paste

Pastes copied/cut text. Within Mosaic, you can paste text into dialog boxes, pop-up window boxes and Annotations. You cannot paste text into a Web document.

## Clear

Deletes selected text. Does not work in Web documents since they cannot be altered.

## Find

Locates text within the currently displayed document. A window pops up asking "What text?" See Figure 3-5.

Three check boxes within the Find window offer search options:

- Case Sensitive
  Matches the upper- and lowercase of the text being searched. For example, with this option selected, a search on "Table" will not find "table."

- Search Backwards
  Searches for a text match prior to the point of your current cursor location.

- Wrap-Around Search
  Searches from the current cursor location to the end of document and then begins the search from the top of the document.

When the text being searched is found, it will be highlighted within the document. It will only highlight the first occurrence of the text.

## Find Again...

Finds multiple occurrences of a word or text string. The Find feature only locates the first occurrence. You need to use Find Again... to find each additional occurrence of the text.

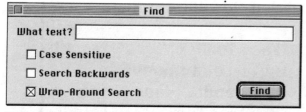

Figure 3-5: *The Mosaic Find window.*

## Show Clipboard

Displays the content of your Macintosh's Clipboard.

 **HOT TIP** — · — · — · — · — · — · — · — · — · — · — ·

Is it a box or is it a window? The difference between a dialog box and a window can sometimes be confusing. In *Mosaic Quick Tour,* the following distinctions are made:

- *Windows* are pop-up screens that can be moved around, opened or closed, overlapped, and placed behind and on top of other windows. Multiple windows can be open at the same time.
- *Dialog boxes* cannot be moved and they will not go away until you interact with them (e.g., entering information or pressing a button). A dialog-type box that is non-interactive (doesn't ask you to do anything) is called a *Message box* (e.g., "Loading... please stand by").

## The Options Menu

The Options menu in Mosaic is one of the most useful menus. It offers several monitoring functions for Web navigation (URL and Status displays, Header Mode) and is used when displaying and moving documents (Load to Disk, Auto-Load Images, Use and Remove Temp files and Flush Cache). It's also where you access the Preferences and Styles windows, which are important for configuring your Web documents and Mosaic itself.

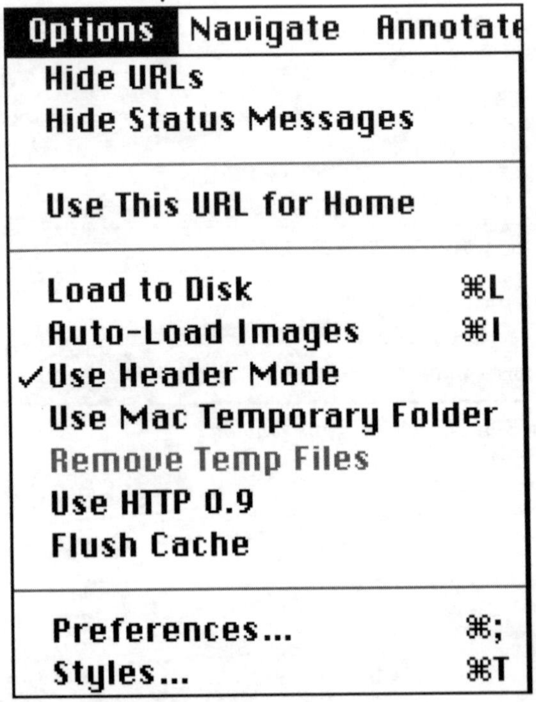

### Hide URLs

Turns the URL display box on and off in the navigation panel. The menu shows Hide URLs when the URL box is visible and Show URLs when it is not.

### Hide Status Messages

Turns the status messages on and off in the navigation panel. Status messages let you know what Web document is currently being looked for, when a connection is being made, the status of the document's transfer, etc.

| Options | Navigate | Annotate |
| --- | --- | --- |
| Hide URLs | | |
| Hide Status Messages | | |
| Use This URL for Home | | |
| Load to Disk | | ⌘L |
| Auto-Load Images | | ⌘I |
| ✓Use Header Mode | | |
| Use Mac Temporary Folder | | |
| Remove Temp Files | | |
| Use HTTP 0.9 | | |
| Flush Cache | | |
| Preferences... | | ⌘; |
| Styles... | | ⌘T |

Figure 3-6: *The Options menu.*

## Use This URL for Home

Allows you to select the current HTML document as your home page each time you launch Mosaic.

To have your own home page displayed each time you start your Mosaic session,

1. Choose Open Local from the File menu.

2. When your page displays, pick Use This URL for Home from the Options menu. This new home page will be automatically copied to your Preferences file. (For instructions on making your own home page, see Chapter 4, "Web Walking With Mosaic.")

## Load to Disk

When checked, tells Mosaic to load documents to disk as you access them. If you've selected this option, whenever you open a new document, either by clicking on a hotlink or by selecting Open URL..., Mosaic brings up a File Save dialog box instead of displaying the document. You select where you want the transferred file to be sent. This option is useful if you want to retrieve, say, a QuickTime movie, and you want to keep it rather than have Mosaic temporarily store it and then dump it when you quit.

## Auto-Load Images

Automatically loads inline images when you open a document that contains them. This dramatically slows down access time over a dial-up SLIP or PPP connection. If Auto-Load Images does not have a check mark by it, it is turned off and the inline image icon is displayed, indicating that an inline image exists.

**Do-It-Yourself Electronic Publishing** The Internet is not only a great place to engage in stimulating conversations and to consume news and information, it can also turn you into a news and information producer. Thousands of Net citizens publish their own electronic newsletters, moderated mailing lists, FAQs and Web documents.

Brock N. Meeks, by day a writer for *Communications Daily*, becomes a one-man wire service by night. He is the creator of *CyberWire Dispatch*, a series of erratically published reports on significant Net happenings, communications law and policy, and freedom of speech issues in cyberspace. Meeks's service is free and his dispatches are serious, in-depth and hard-hitting. *CyberWire Dispatch* has been mentioned in a number of magazines and dailies, including *The New York Times*, *The Washington Post*, and *Wired* magazine. The *Dispatch* can be delivered directly to your email box by sending mail to majordomo@cyberwerks.com with "subscribe cwd-l" as the first line of your message. To access *CyberWire Dispatch* on the Web, send a URL to http://cyberwerks.com:70/1/cyberwire. Back issues are available in gopherspace from gopher cyberwerks.com. →

To view inline images, simply click on the  icon. The image will be transferred and displayed.

## Use Header Mode

Provides additional information about a link before you connect to it. The information includes file type, file size and server information and appears in a pop-up window. This is a new feature of Mosaic 2.x. See Figure 3-7.

## Use Mac Temporary Folder

When checked, stores all temporary files where you've told Mosaic to put them (as indicated in the Preferences window). If unchecked, stores all temporary files in your System Folder.

## Remove Temp Files

Deletes temporary files while you are still in Mosaic (otherwise, temp files are automatically deleted when you quit the program).

## Use HTTP 0.9

Allows Mosaic to use an older version of HTTP (HyperText Transport Protocol). There are few (if any) HTTP servers running 0.9, but NCSA keeps this option available just in case you encounter one.

## Flush Cache

Flushes all documents and images contained in the cache. Mosaic stores all recently accessed documents so that it doesn't have to go back to the server to get the files again. This command deletes all those cached files.

Jon Lebkowsky and Paco Xander Nathan, both well-known Net personalities, are quickly becoming mini-media moguls. Several years ago, they started FringeWare, a company and Net community, dedicated to creating an alternative marketplace for goods and services offered by Net citizens. They now maintain a conference on The WELL BBS, publish a Net-based catalog, moderate a mailing list on alternative community and do-it-yourself technology, and publish two print magazines: *FringeWare Review* and *Unshaved Truths*. And—if that wasn't enough—they have day jobs! The FringeWare Home Page is located at http://io.com/commercial/fringeware/home.html

These are just two examples of successful Net-based publishing efforts. There are countless others. As you delve deeper into the Web, you'll find many new and exciting forms of media.

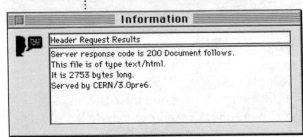

Figure 3-7: *The Header Mode window.*

### Preferences...

Brings up the main Preferences window. See "Configuring Preferences" on page 41 for how to set up your preferences.

### Styles...

Brings up the main type styles window. From here you can control the way type looks in your Mosaic documents. See "Using Styles in Mosaic" on page 53 for more information.

## The Navigate Menu

Mosaic includes many menu, command key and icono-graphic options for navigating the Web. The Navigate menu (see Figure 3-8) offers many of the same features found in the navigation panel of the Mosaic window as well as a list of useful Web locations.

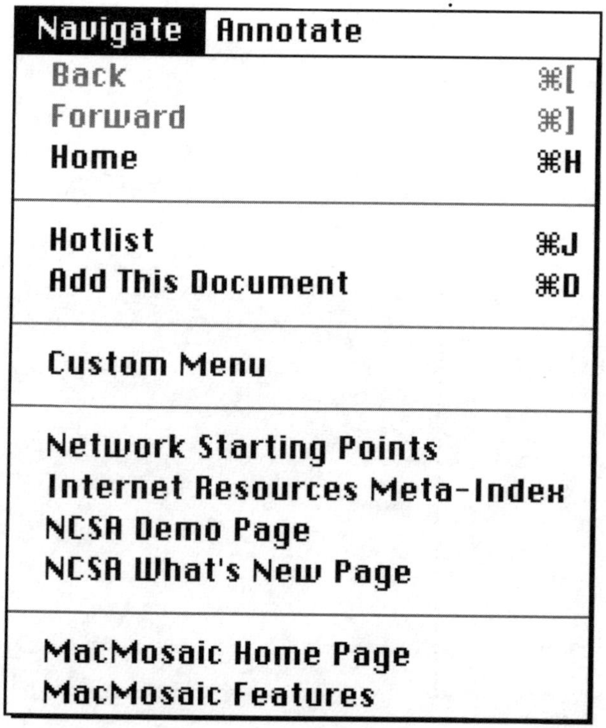

### Back

Lets you move back through the documents you visited most recently. Back stays dimmed until you have a previous page to return to.

### Forward

Lets you move forward through the pages you visited during your current Mosaic session. Only works if you have been back through pages and then decided to move forward again. Stays dimmed until you have a forward page to move to.

### Home

Takes you back to your home page, which, if you're using the defaulted home page, is the NCSA server. Home can

| Navigate | Annotate | |
|----------|----------|---|
| Back | | ⌘[ |
| Forward | | ⌘] |
| Home | | ⌘H |
| Hotlist | | ⌘J |
| Add This Document | | ⌘D |
| Custom Menu | | |
| Network Starting Points | | |
| Internet Resources Meta-Index | | |
| NCSA Demo Page | | |
| NCSA What's New Page | | |
| MacMosaic Home Page | | |
| MacMosaic Features | | |

Figure 3-8: *The Navigate menu.*

be a comforting place to return to if you get hopelessly tangled in Webspace.

## Hotlist

Pops up a Hotlist Items window where you can manage a series of *hotlists*. Hotlists are like address books for the World Wide Web. You can keep a number of lists, named as you choose (business, fun, technical, whatever). Any Web documents you want quick and easy access to can be added to a hotlist. See "How to Use Hotlists" on page 60 for more information.

## Add This Document

Adds the currently displayed document's URL to your currently selected hotlist.

## Custom Menu

Allows you to build custom pull-down menus.

## Network Starting Points

Takes you to the Network Starting Points page at NCSA. If you have read this *Quick Tour* and are ready to do some serious Web walking, this is a good place to start.

## Internet Resources Meta-Index

Lists NCSA's valuable Internet resources.

## NCSA Demo Page

Provides an interactive tour of Mosaic's capabilities and a series of hotlinks to exemplary Web documents.

## NCSA What's New Page

Opens NCSA's frequently updated list of news and new offerings on the Web. One of the most popular stopping off points on the Web. Kind of like a town bulletin board or kiosk.

Figure 3-9: *The Annotate menu.*

## MacMosaic Home Page

Connects you to the home page of the Web server at NCSA, the official home page for Mac Mosaic.

## MacMosaic Features

Introduces the features, capabilities and bugs in the various versions of Mac Mosaic. To find out about the latest releases and fixes for Mosaic 2.x, check out this document.

## The Annotate Menu

Lets you access both written and audio versions of *Annotations*. Annotations are like personal post-it notes that you can attach to a Web document. See Figure 3-9.

### Text...

Opens an Annotation window (see Figure 3-10) where you can add personal notes to the Web page currently being displayed. Your name (if you entered it in the Preferences: Misc window) automatically appears in the name box.

To add an annotation,

1. Enter a title for your note in the Title box.

2. Type your note in the scrollable text box provided.

3. When your note is complete, hit OK. Your annotation will appear at the bottom of the document as a hotlink.

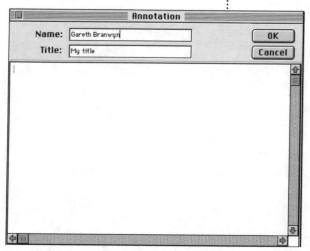

Figure 3-10: *The text Annotation window.*

## Audio...

Lets you attach spoken notes to a document.

To create an audio annotation,

1. Choose Audio... from the Annotate menu. A window will pop up (see Figure 3-11).

2. Enter your name (if not already defaulted) and the title of your audio note.

3. Hit the Record button. A standard Mac recording dialog box (see Figure 3-12) will appear. Consult your *Macintosh User's Guide* if you are unsure how to use the recorder.

4. When you are satisfied with your audio notation, press Save.

5. The title of the new audio notation will appear at the end of the current document.

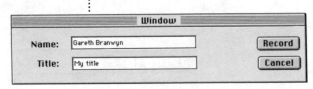

Figure 3-11: *Audio Annotate window.*

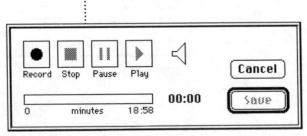

Figure 3-12: *The Record dialog box.*

## Edit annotation

Allows editing of text annotations only. This command brings up the original annotation. Once you've made your text changes, choose Reload from the File menu and the changes take effect immediately.

## Delete annotation

Allows you to delete annotations (both text and audio). The deletion will not take effect immediately. The hotlink continues to appear on the page until the next time Mosaic downloads this document. If you want the deletion to take effect immediately, select Reload from the File menu.

*Note: Annotations are personal and cannot be accessed by anyone else on the Internet. They are stored on your hard drive and are not made part of the HTML documents you are viewing.*

## Balloon Help Menu

The System 7 Balloon Help feature does not work in Mosaic (who uses it anyway?), but under this icon you can find a series of tutorial documents. See Figure 3-13.

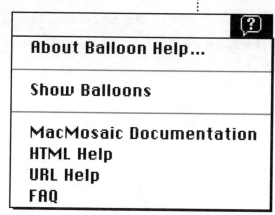

Figure 3-13: *The Balloon Help menu in Mosaic.*

### MacMosaic Documentation

Contains an online user's guide prepared by the developers at NCSA.

### HTML Help

Gives a basic rundown of what HTML is and how it works within Mosaic and on the World Wide Web.

### URL Help

Introduces you to URLs (Uniform Resource Locators), the addressing standard on the Web.

### FAQ

Lists the current version of Mosaic's Frequently Asked Questions file.

## Configuring Preferences

The Preferences area in Mosaic 2.x divides preference features into four categories:

- Misc—General Preferences (email address, home page).
- Links—Hotlinks, hotlink colors and Global History information.
- Dirs—Setting up storage areas on your hard drive for Mosaic files and configuring Helper Applications.
- Gates—Gateway information to network servers.

These icons are located on the left-hand side of the Preferences window. A click on each icon brings up its window. See Figure 3-14.

## Configuring the Items in Misc

1. In the Home Page box, enter the URL you want to use as your home page (where you want Mosaic to go first when you launch it). It is defaulted to the NCSA server.
2. Enter your User Name (or whatever name you want to appear in your personal Annotations and when sending email to the Mosaic developers).
3. In the EMail Address box, enter your full email address in the form of username@site.domain.

If you want to change the Background Color of your Mosaic documents,

4. Click on the Background Color box. A standard Mac color wheel dialog box will appear. See Figure 3-15.

5. Select the new color you want and choose OK. For your new color choice to be implemented, you need to choose Apply in the main Misc window. When you return to the current document, the new color will appear. Experiment until you get a color choice you like. If you are unsure how to use the color wheel, consult your *Macintosh User's Guide*.

## Configuring the Items in Links

To view the Links window (see Figure 3-16), click on the Links icon located on the left-hand side of the main Preferences window.

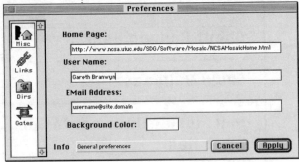

Figure 3-14: *Main Preferences window.*

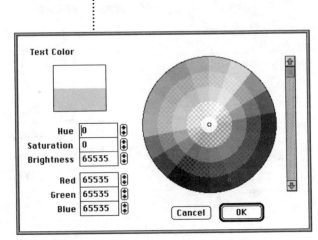

Figure 3-15: *The Macintosh Color Wheel.*

## Underline Hotlinks

Underlines all hotlinks (links between one Web document and another) for greater visibility.

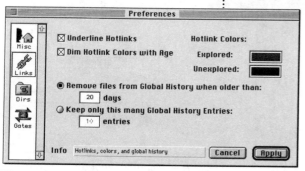

Figure 3-16: *The Links Preferences window.*

*Note: Hotlinks were called Anchor Colors in MacMosaic 1.x. They are also referred to as the more widely used Hyperlinks.*

## Dim Hotlink Colors with Age

Fades Hotlink colors from the Explored color to the Unexplored color over the time period specified.

## Hotlink Colors

Indicates the hotlink colors assigned to Explored and Unexplored hotlinks. The default colors are Red for explored links and Blue for unexplored links. To change these colors, click on the color box for the hotlink color you wish to change. A color wheel will pop up. Select the new hotlink color and click on OK. You also need to click on the Apply button in the main Links preferences window. When you return to the current Mosaic window, your new hotlink color choices will be visible.

## Remove files from Global History...

Specifies a time period before documents will be removed from the global history list. Global History is a new feature of Mosaic 2.x that maintains a history of your explored hotlinks between sessions.

## Keep only this many Global History Entries

Specifies the number of history entries that Mosaic will save in your Global History list.

*Note: You can only choose one of these two options, not both.*

## Configuring the Items in Dirs

To view the Dirs preferences window (see Figure 3-17), click on the Dirs icon located on the left-hand side of the main Preferences window.

The Dirs (Directories) window lets you select the destination directories for files saved during your Mosaic sessions. There is also a button for accessing the area where you configure your Helper Applications (additional programs Mosaic needs to manage media files such as movies and graphics).

### Set Temp Directory

Stores files in a temporary location. When you ask Mosaic to transfer a file that requires a Helper Application, the file is temporarily saved to your hard drive. The default destination is your System Folder. To Set Temp Directory (if you don't want these items stored in the default location),

1. Press the Set Temp Directory button.

2. A standard Mac dialog box appears asking where you want the Temporary Directory to be put. Choose the desired location and then press the Select <Folder Name> button.

### Set Hotlist Directory

Allows you to specify the folder where Mosaic will store your hotlists. See the "How to Use Hotlists" section on page 59.

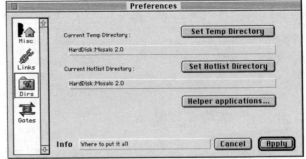

Figure 3-17: *The Dirs Preferences window.*

### Helper applications...

Brings up the Helper Application settings window. Helper applications are external programs that Mosaic uses to access media files (sounds, graphics, movies) on the Web. See the "Configuring Helper Applications" section on page 46 for more information.

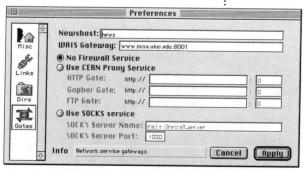

Figure 3-18: *The Gates Preferences window.*

## Configuring the Items in Gates

The Gates window is where you specify gateways to other Net services such as USENET Newsgroups and the WAIS (Wide-Area Information Servers) system. See Figure 3-18.

### Newshost

Allows you to read Usenet News with Mosaic after you enter the address of your newshost (if you plan on reading Usenet News in Mosaic). Ask your service provider for the newshost address at their location.

### WAIS Gateway

Defaults to the NCSA WAIS gateway. If you have a local gateway, enter it here. Ask your service provider for more details. Mosaic can't handle WAIS data directly; therefore, it must go through a gateway that translates the data so that Mosaic can access it.

### No Firewall Service

Processes network input and output and allows the computers on a LAN to pretend that they're actually on the Net when they (technically) aren't. This is the default selection (used unless your system is on a firewall service). See "What in Blue Blazes Is a Firewall?" on the next page for more details.

## Use CERN Proxy Service & Use SOCKS Service

Mosaic 2.0 supports both CERN proxy and SOCKS services.

*Note: The Preferences file in 2.x is incompatible with 1.x. Because of this, you can't jump between versions on the same computer and then try to save your preferences for each. 2.x will override 1.x's settings.*

## Configuring Helper Applications

Helper Applications are perhaps the most unituitive part of Mosaic. Helper Applications windows, commands and terminology look intimidating to the average user. But fear not. If you're lucky you'll probably need to do little in this area. Your main task is to make sure all the basic Helper Applications are on your hard drive.

Helper Applications are external programs that Mosaic uses to help it display various media files. This scheme allows Mosaic to keep its mind on its business, while letting other sophisticated viewing and listening applications handle the media presentations. This also gives Mosaic a great degree of flexibility, allowing you to add new types of Helper Applications as you need them. The first thing you need to do is check to see which of the Helper Applications you have and which you'll need. Table 3-1 shows you the default applications Mosaic uses.

**What in Blue Blazes Is a Firewall?** A firewall is a server computer that is set up between the users of a local-area network (or LAN) and their gateway to the Internet. As you might imagine, because the Internet is public, it is not very secure. Every computer on the Internet is considered a peer of every other computer. A computer attached to a LAN that is routed to the Internet is potentially accessible to anyone on the Net. A firewall processes network input and output and allows the computers on a LAN to pretend that they're actually on the Net when they (technically) aren't. The problem with this scheme is that it sometimes hinders the performance of programs that want to be directly Net-connected. Mosaic is such a program. The CERN Proxy/SOCKS services, now available with Mosaic 2.x, help improve gateway performance for systems that are hiding behind firewalls.

| File Type | Default Application | Payment Type |
|-----------|--------------------|--------------|
| GIF/JPEG (images) | JPEGView | Postcardware |
| TIFF (images) | GIFConverter | Shareware |
| QuickTime (movies) | SimplePlayer | Comes w/QT |
| MPEG (movies) | Sparkle | Freeware |
| AU (sounds) | SoundMachine | Freeware |
| BinHexed (files) | StuffIt Expander | Freeware |

Table 3-1: *The default Helper Applications.*

All of these programs (except SimplePlayer) are freeware or shareware and are available via anonymous FTP from sumex-aim.stanford.edu, mac.archive.umich.edu and many of the other FTP sites listed elsewhere in this book. (See Table 2-2 in Chapter 2 for other FTP site listings.) SimplePlayer is an Apple product and is not public domain. If you don't already have it, you can download it free of charge from the NCSA FTP site (ftp.ncsa.uiuc.edu).

After you've downloaded and unpacked all the Helper Applications you didn't already have, you're probably done. When you encounter a media file during a Mosaic session and download it, Mosaic accesses the appropriate helper and uses it to open the file. When done viewing or listening, you can quit the Helper Application (which is now on top of Mosaic) or you can save the file to disk, if that option is available.

If you wish to change any of the Helper Applications or add or remove applications, you'll need to go to the Helper configuration window accessed via the Dirs icon in the Preferences window.

For example, let's say you want to change an application. Mosaic is defaulted to access SimplePlayer for running QuickTime movies. If you didn't have SimplePlayer, but had another QT movie viewer, such as BijouPlay, here's how you would configure Mosaic to use the new application:

1. Select the Preferences... command from the Options menu and click on the Dirs icon.

2. Click on the Helper applications... button. The window seen in Figure 3-19 will appear.

3. Scroll down the Document Type -> Application window until you see video/quicktime -> SimplePlayer. See Figure 3-20.

4. Click on the Set Application... button. A standard open file dialog box will appear. Find the folder that contains the application (in this case BijouPlay) and click the Open button.

5. If your selected application has a character file type (or several) built into it, you'll get the type of dialog box seen in Figure 3-21.

6. Move along the horizontal scroll bar until you find the Mac file type you're looking for, select it and click OK. The new application has been added to the list in the Document type -> Application window. (See steps 8 and 9 below for an explanation of the check boxes.)

7. If Mosaic cannot read the four-character Mac file type (which happens with BijouPlay, for instance), a different dialog box pops up asking you to manually enter the four-character file type (see Figure 3-22). Since BijouPlay is a QuickTime player, you would type in MOOV and then press OK. The new application has been added to the list in the Document type -> Application window. (See steps 8 and 9 below for an explanation of the check boxes.)

See Table 3-2 for a listing of the four-character file types that are used in Mosaic Helper Applications.

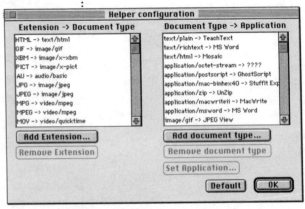

Figure 3-19: *Helper configuration window.*

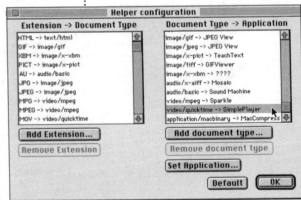

Figure 3-20: *Selecting SimplePlayer.*

If you attempt set a new Helper Application and Mosaic cannot read the four-character designation for the application's file type, it will ask you to type it in manually. This doesn't happen very often (only when the application was made by a lazy programmer!) If it does happen, and you need to know the four-character file name, Table 3-2 lists the most common ones.

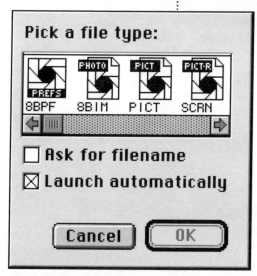

Figure 3-21: *Pick a file type dialog box.*

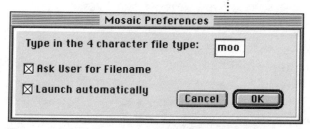

Figure 3-22: *The manual entry file type dialog box.*

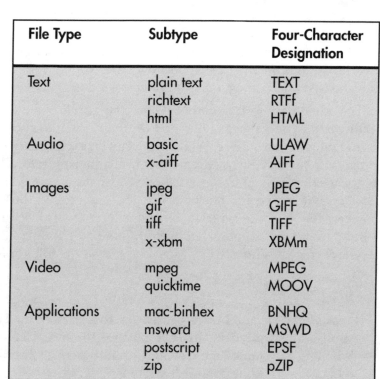

| File Type | Subtype | Four-Character Designation |
|---|---|---|
| Text | plain text | TEXT |
| | richtext | RTFf |
| | html | HTML |
| Audio | basic | ULAW |
| | x-aiff | AIFf |
| Images | jpeg | JPEG |
| | gif | GIFF |
| | tiff | TIFF |
| | x-xbm | XBMm |
| Video | mpeg | MPEG |
| | quicktime | MOOV |
| Applications | mac-binhex | BNHQ |
| | msword | MSWD |
| | postscript | EPSF |
| | zip | pZIP |

Table 3-2: *Four-character file types for Mosaic Helper Applications.*

8. If you want Mosaic to always save this media file type, check the Ask User for Filename box. Then, each time you download this type of file to Mosaic (QuickTime movies in our example), a standard File Save dialog box pops up asking you where you want to put the file and what you want to name it. Obviously, you can dismiss this dialog box for any files you don't want to save.

9. If you want Mosaic to launch the media file as soon as it's finished transferring it, check the Launch automatically box. Since few people want to save most of the media files they access through Mosaic, the default options on all of the applications are Ask User for Filename is not checked and Launch automatically is checked.

The other main feature of the Helper configuration window is the ability to add new types of files and to "map" them to applications found on your hard drive. While this is not an exceedingly difficult procedure, since the new Mosaic user probably won't need this capability, it's not covered in this guide. If you do find yourself needing to add a new file type and one of its applications, consult the Configuring Viewers for New File Types in the online MacMosaic Documentation (found under the Balloon Help menu). Table 3-3 lists all of the File Types currently supported by Mosaic and their default applications.

**HOT TIP** — · — · — · — · — · — · — · — · — · — · — · — · —

Pressing the Default button causes you to lose all of the Helper Applications you've added. (For instance, if I press Default after switching the QuickTime viewing application from SimplePlayer to BijouPlay, Mosaic defaults back to SimplePlayer.)

| File Type | Subtype | Application |
|---|---|---|
| Text | plain text | TeachText |
| | richtext | MS Word |
| | html | Mosaic |
| Audio | basic | SoundMachine |
| | x-aiff | Mosaic |
| Images | jpeg | JPEGViewer |
| | gif | JPEGViewer |
| | tiff | GIFConverter |
| | x-xbm | (no default application) |
| Video | mpeg | Sparkle |
| | quicktime | SimplePlayer |
| Applications | octect-stream | (no default application) |
| | mac-binhex | StuffIt Expander |
| | macbinary | MacCompress |
| | macwriteii | MacWrite II |
| | msword | Microsoft Word |
| | postscript | GhostScript |
| | zip | UnZip |

Table 3-3: *Files types and Helper Applications in Mosaic.*

*Note: When you make changes to Helper Applications in Mosaic, you'll see the change in the Document Type -> Application list, but the actual application change will not take effect until you quit your current Mosaic session and re-launch.*

When you first open up Mosaic, you automatically go the Mosaic
Home Page at NCSA. Due to the current popularity of Mosaic,
traffic to the NCSA server is high. You can ease this burden on the
electronic highways by making another Web location the default
home page. Simply change the Home Page box in the Preferences
window (under Misc). Or you can use Mosaic 2.x's new feature
called Use This URL for Home. Simply go to the home page you
wish to select as your new starting point (Ventana's Visitor Center
at http://www.vmedia.com, for instance). Once you arrive,
choose the Use This URL for Home menu option. Your new home
will be automatically registered in the appropriate box in the
Preferences window under Misc.

## Using Styles in Mosaic

The Styles... feature in Mosaic allows you to customize the
look of the Web documents you view. Here's where you
get to be a little creative, changing fonts to suit your fancy,
making text bigger or smaller, or changing font colors. See
Figure 3-23.

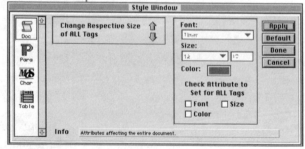

Figure 3-23: *The Style Window (with the Doc settings
selected).*

To change any of the default type settings in Mosaic,
open the Style window by selecting Styles... from the
Options Menu. A window, similar to the one for Preferences, appears. The icons on the left are used to switch
between screens covering documents (Doc), paragraphs
(Para), characters (Char) and tables (Table). These are the four types of
HTML styles that can be customized in Mosaic. You can tell which
section is currently selected by looking for a black box around one of

the icons. As each icon is selected, a window of information relevant to that style appears to its right.

### The Document Settings

The Document settings are visible after clicking on the Doc icon at the top of the icon bar. Chances are, when you first go to Styles... Doc will already be selected. See Figure 3-23.

### Change Respective Size of ALL Tags

Allows you to do a global size change of all the text that appears in the document window. To do a global size change, click on either the up (bigger text) or down (smaller text) arrows located in the Change Respective Size of ALL Tags box.

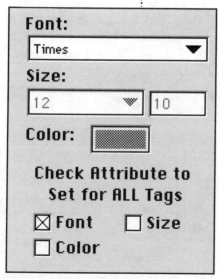

Figure 3-24: *The Font styles box.*

### Changing Font, Font Size & Font Color

The "global" font style in Mosaic will be defaulted to whatever you set here. So, if you want to see everything in, say, Palatino rather than Times (the current default setting), you would

1. Click on the Font check box (see Figure 3-24) located to the right of the Doc window. The Font pull-down menu at the top of the box will un-dim.

2. Hold down the mouse button with your cursor inside the Font window to see a pull-down menu of all the available fonts.

3. Select the font you want to be the new default font (in this case Palatino).

4. Likewise, you can change the font size by checking the font Size box and then selecting a new font size from the pull-down menu in the Size box.

5. To change the font color, click in the Color check box. Then, by clicking inside the un-dimmed Color box, a standard Macintosh color wheel will appear. Choose your new color. If you are unsure how to use the color wheel, consult your *Macintosh User's Guide*.

6. When you've finalized your changes, click the Apply button on the right side of the Doc window and your style changes take effect immediately.

By moving the Style window to the side of your screen, you can see the changes taking place in any of the Style windows when you hit Apply.

If you really mess up and want things to return to normal, click the Default button. You can also Cancel at any time during your styles experimenting and return to your current document without changing anything.

7. Finally, once you're satisfied with your changes, click the Done button to save all of your changes and to exit the Style windows.

## The Paragraph Settings

Clicking on the Paragraphs icon (located directly below the Documents icon) brings up a whole new screen of style settings. These settings handle the way Mosaic formats various style elements ("tags") in HTML documents (headers, quotations, lists, tables, etc). See Figure 3-25.

To view the main menu of paragraph items that can be changed in this window, hold down the cursor in the box labeled HTML Style. A pop-up menu of Paragraph elements appears.

**A Little Background on HTML** HyperText Markup Language (HTML) is a specialized set of "tags" that tells Mosaic (and other Web browsers) how to display the text, hotlinks, images and other multimedia elements you see on your screen. These tags are guidelines for how a browser should display the material. Some tags are required by all HTML browsers, while other tags are optional. All Web browsers are different. Some, like Mosaic, are graphical, while others are text-based. Since HTML is only a set of guidelines for displaying the documents, not everyone has to have the same capabilities to access Web information. Once the HTML document arrives at its destination, the browsing soft →

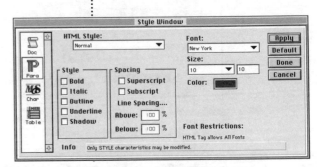

Figure 3-25: *The paragraph Style Window.*

The concept of style elements will be familiar to anyone who has used styles within a word processing or page layout program. They are a way of controlling the formatting within a document so that documents appear with the same consistent typography. So, for instance, if you always want the first level headings (Header 1) in your documents to be displayed in 24-point Helvetica, you would do the following:

ware can use whatever tags are appropriate to it and ignore the rest. For instance, Lynx, another popular Web browser, supports text only. It therefore ignores the HTML style information that's not relevant to it. Mosaic, on the other hand, presents documents in all their multimedia glory and even gives you further display options. This flexibility allows you to change the way Web documents look on your system.

For more information on how HTML works, check out the following Web documents:
The HTML Primer at
http://www.ncsa.uiuc.edu/General/Internet/WWW/HTMLPrimer.html
HTML Documentation at
http://www.ucc.ie/info/net/htmldoc.html

1. Hold down the cursor again in the box labeled HTML Style.

2. When the menu pops up, slide the cursor along the list until Header 1 is highlighted. Let go of the mouse button.

3. Select Helvetica from the Font menu and the number 24 from the Size menu.

4. Click on Apply. You will see that the first header in your Mosaic document window has now changed to Helvetica 24 point.

Table 3-4 lists the types of Paragraph tags that can be changed in this window. One nifty feature of Mosaic 2.x is that the Info box at the bottom of each Style window tells you if any of the tags you've selected have restrictions on what attributes can be changed. For instance, selecting the paragraph element "List Items" from the HTML Styles menu, the Info box informs you that "Only STYLE characteristics may be modified." Alternately, choosing "Address" from the menu, the Info window says, "All characteristics may be modified." There is also a box called Font Restrictions that lets you know if the paragraph tag you've selected has any restrictions on font type or size.

| Style Type | What It Modifies |
|---|---|
| Normal | The default paragraph style |
| Header 1 | Topmost heading |
| Header 2 | Second level heading |
| Header 3 | Third level heading |
| Header 4 | Fourth level heading |
| Header 5 | Fifth level heading |
| Header 6 | Sixth level heading |
| Address | How the author's name and email address will appear at the bottom of documents |
| Blockquote | Extended or block quotations |
| Preformatted | Text already formatted in monospaced font (i.e., program listings) |
| Typewriter | Character style in monospaced font |
| Bullet List | List in bullet form |
| Definitions | Contents of a definition (one line only) |
| Directory List | List in directory form |
| Menu List | List in menu form |
| Numeric List | List of numbers |
| List Item | List in hierarchical form |
| Definition Term | Style of term to be defined |
| Definition Paragraph | Contents of a definition (paragraph) |
| Paragraph Break | Line spacing between paragraphs |
| Line Break | Spacing between lines |
| Form | Style elements for fill-in-the-blank forms |

Table 3-4: *Paragraph style tags.*

By selecting each one of these, the Info and Font Restrictions boxes tell you which of the attributes (style, spacing, font, size, color) can or cannot be modified.

Let's try a few more examples to make this clearer.

If you want all information that has been tagged within an HTML document as the style Definition Term to always appear in bold face and the color red, you would make those selections in this window and apply them (using the same method outlined above). From then on, whenever a document appeared that included definitions, the actual term would appear in bold/red. (You would need to choose Definitions to change attributes of the definition itself.)

If you want all bulleted lists in your documents to appear underlined, you would choose Bullet List from the HTML Style menu and then click on the Underline box.

Keep in mind that these changes will only affect styles that have been appropriately tagged by the document's creator. If an HTML document creator decides not to tag a definition term as a Definition Term, your modifications will have no effect.

## The Character Settings

Clicking on the Character icon (located directly below the Paragraph icon) brings up the style settings (see Figure 3-26) that affect individual characters or types of words (citations, examples, computer code). If you pull down the HTML style menu, you'll see the following choices:

Bold
Italic
Underline

**Postcardware**   Most people familiar with computer and online culture are familiar with Freeware (software, like Mosaic, that's distributed free of charge) and Shareware (software that's distributed freely, but you're supposed to pay for it if you use it). So what's Postcardware? It's when the creator of an application only asks that you write and tell them what you think about their creation. Postcardware is what Aaron Giles, creator of the popular JPEGView, uses as his means of compensation. If you use JPEGview on a regular basis, you're obliged to send Giles a postcard. Having once been a devout mail artist, and still having an obsession with getting cool mail everyday, I can relate to Aaron's rather eccentric form of payment. →

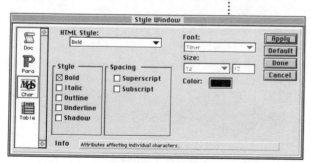

Figure 3-26: *Character Style Window.*

Citation
Emphasis
Example
Listing
Strong
Variable
Code
Keyboard
Plain Text
Sample

This all starts to get a little confusing, and you may have a hard time figuring out the difference between this section and the Paragraph style section. Here are some examples of how Character Styles would be used.

If you disliked italic and wanted to make sure that all italic text in Mosaic documents is changed to bold, you would make that change in the Character window. You would

1. Choose Italic from the HTML Style box.

2. Click on the Bold check box.

3. Click on the Apply button.

Now, whenever you access a document that has been tagged with italic text, it will be changed to bold face.

*Note: In the Character style window you will notice that type size, color and font are all dimmed out. These attributes are not changeable in this window.*

Given how great JPEGView is, and the fact that it's one of the default external viewers for Mosaic, I hope he's getting LOTS of great postcards (hint, hint). Here's one that I sent him recently:

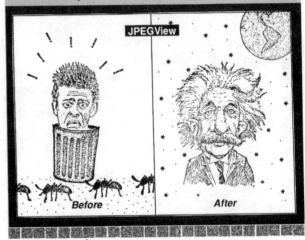

## The Table Settings

The final Style window (Table) is where you can make changes to how Mosaic displays tables and the data within those tables (see Figure 3-27). If you pull down on the HTML Style menu you'll see these choices:

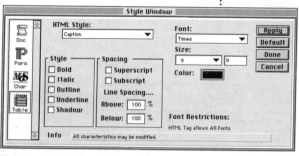

Caption
Data
Header
Table

The Table styles work the same as the styles in the previous three windows. To change attributes on any of the four table elements (Caption, Data, Header, Table),

Figure 3-27: *The table Style Window.*

1. Select the style you want to change in the HTML Style box.

2. Choose the desired new attributes.

3. Click Apply to save the changes.

4. Look at the changes in the main Mosaic document window. If you're not satisfied, you can change the attributes further or choose Default and return all table style attributes to their default settings.

## How to Use Hotlists

There are so many great resources to discover in the Web. In an average Mosaic session you can open up oodles of documents, explore dozens of hotlinks and generally tangle yourself up into knots. One of the most useful parts of Mosaic is Hotlists, the feature that enables you to create multiple "address books" of documents you've visited that you might want to come back to. You can save these lists under different names, import and export lists into your hotlists menu and even exchange lists with other Mosaic users.

## Creating Your First Hotlist

1. Go to the document you wish to put into your Hotlist menu.

2. Select Add This Document, found under the Navigate menu (or use Command+D). A dialog box will ask you to name the hotlist.

3. Type in the name and press Save.

4. Now, every time during this session you want to add a Web document to *this* hotlist, all you have to do is press Command+D and it will automatically be added.

## How to Create a New Hotlist

1. Open up the Hotlist Items window located under the Navigate menu. The Hotlist Items window will appear with the current hotlist selected (in this case Hotlist.1). See Figure 3-28.

2. Select New HL from the row of buttons along the bottom. A new hotlist called Untitled Hotlist will appear. Go back to the main Mosaic screen and find the Web document you wish to add to this new list.

3. Press Command+D and a File Save dialog box will appear. Name your new hotlist and press Save.

4. To switch back and forth between your multiple lists, click on the list name field above the list window and the titles of the other hotlists you have created will pop up. Select the list you want to activate.

## Using a Hotlist

1. Select the Hotlist menu item under Navigate. The Hotlist Items window will appear (as seen in Figure 3-28).

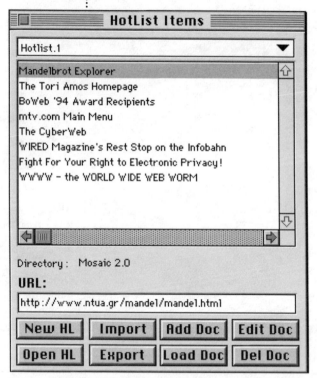

Figure 3-28: *The Hotlist Items window.*

2. Click and hold in the hotlist title field until all the list titles are visible (assuming you have more than one list).

3. Slide the cursor up or down the title list until the list you want is highlighted. Let go of the mouse button. The desired list will appear in the main window of the Hotlist Items window.

4. Find the Web document name you wish to access. Double-clicking on the document name opens the connection to the site where that document is stored. Notice that the document's URL appears in the window at the bottom of the list window.

## Opening a Hotlist

If you have a hotlist that is not in the folder in which Mosaic looks for hotlists (as specified in Preferences under the Dirs icon), you can open that list by doing the following:

1. Click on the Open HL button from the row of buttons along the bottom of the Hotlist Items window.

2. A standard Mac Find File dialog box will appear. When you find the hotlist you wish to add, double-click to load it into your Hotlists menu.

*Note: When you quit out of Mosaic, the list that you have added from outside the selected hotlist directory will not be in your hotlists menu the next time you launch Mosaic. Only those lists that are stored in the specified hotlist directory (as entered in Preferences: Dirs) will appear in your hotlist menu.*

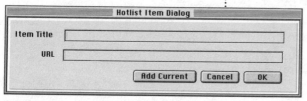

Figure 3-29: *The Hotlist Item Dialog box.*

## Manually Adding a Document

If you wish to manually add a document to a hotlist,

1. Click on the Add Doc button on the Hotlist Items window. A data entry window will appear. See Figure 3-29.

2. Type in the title of the document and the document's URL. Whenever entering URLs by hand, make sure you enter them correctly.

3. When you are done, click OK and your new document will be added to the current hotlist.

4. If you wish to access the document you just entered, press the Load Doc button on the Hotlist Items window and Mosaic will immediately connect to that site.

## Editing a Document

If you get a URL address incorrect or want to change its name,

1. Select the item in the hotlist you want to edit.

2. Click on the Edit Doc button. The same type of window as that used for adding documents will appear (see Figure 3-29).

3. Make your changes and then click OK.

## Deleting Items Within a Hotlist

Select the item you wish to delete by clicking on its name in the Hotlist Items window. Choose Del Doc from the panel of buttons on the bottom of the window. The item will be deleted.

## Deleting an Entire Hotlist

On your hard drive find the Hotlist icon for the file you wish to delete (see Figure 3-30). It will be located in the folder where your hotlists are stored (as specified in Preferences under Dirs). Drag the file to be deleted into the Trash. When you go back to Mosaic, that hotlist no longer appears in your hotlist menu. If you don't want to destroy the list, but you no longer want it to appear in your hotlist menu, just drag it out of the folder where it's stored. You can always use Open HL to access a list during a specific Mosaic session.

Hotlist.1

Figure 3-30: *Hotlist file icon.*

# Navigation in Mosaic

Obviously the reason you're in Mosaic is to go places—to explore that expanding universe of hypermedia we rattled on about in Chapter 1.

Figure 3-31: *Mosaic's navigation panel.*

The main controls for doing this are located in the navigation panel at the top of the Mosaic window. After you've entered in your destination, this panel tells you where you're going, what your trip progress is and gives you the options of retracing your steps or instantly returning home.

## The Title Bar

Displays the title of the current document and also contains the close window box and the zoom box.

*Note: If you only have one Mosaic window open and you close it, you'll need to choose New Window from the File menu to get another window up. The New Window command will open a home page.*

## The Mosaic Status Indicator

The planet icon in the upper left-hand corner of the panel is called the Status Indicator. When Mosaic is searching for a URL or otherwise involved in a data transfer, the Status Indicator becomes animated, with little "lights" zooming around the S-shaped cables. The indicator also changes depending on what it's doing. A document icon means it's transferring text, a filmstrip indicates a movie, a speaker indicates an audio clip, and so forth.

Figure 3-32: *The Status Indicator.*

The Status Indicator can also be used for canceling a document transfer. If, in the middle of a download, you decide that you don't want to continue, simply click on the animated Status Indicator and the transfer will be terminated.

## The Status Message Area

This area, directly below the Status Indicator, displays messages about what's happening during your session when Mosaic is connecting to a site, downloading documents or having trouble with a transfer. These messages can be turned on or off in the Options menu (Show Status Messages). See Figure 3-33.

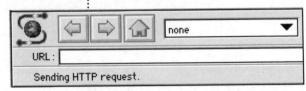

Figure 3-33: *The status message area.*

## The Back Button

Located to the right of the Status Indicator are the Back and Next buttons. The Back button (the arrow pointing to the left) takes you back through all the documents you've accessed during your session. If there are no previous documents loaded, this button will be grayed out.

## The Next Button

The Next button (the arrow pointing to the right) takes you forward to any documents that are "ahead" in the documents that have already been loaded. This button is only available if there are forward documents available (documents that you've accessed during your session, but then moved back through the document queue).

## Home

Pressing this icon at any time during your Mosaic session takes you back to your designated home page. If you have not changed your home page in the Preferences window, pressing Home takes you back to the Web server at NCSA. You can easily change your home page by going to the document you wish to establish as home and then choosing Use This URL for Home (located under the Options menu).

*Note: Back, Next and Home are also available under the Navigate menu. They work exactly the same as their button equivalents.*

## History

The white box to the immediate left of the Home icon is where the history of your most recently viewed Web pages can be accessed. The current document's name is always visible in this box.

### To View the History List

1. Click in the History window and hold the mouse button down. A list of recently viewed documents will pop up. See Figure 3-34.

Figure 3-34: *History list.*

2. From the current page, indicated by a black dot in front of it, slide your cursor up or down the list to select the document you want to view again.

3. Letting go of the mouse takes you back to that document.

## Search

Lets you search through online indices of documents. This is different than the Find command (located under the Edit menu), which only looks within the current document for specified text matches. Search looks through an index of documents for your key word and then presents you with a hotlinked list of the relevant items the search has uncovered. From this list, you can click on any of the linked documents to view them. See Figure 3-35.

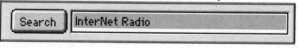

Figure 3-35: *The search box.*

## The URL Box

Shows you the URL of the document you are currently viewing. In version 2.x of Mosaic you can now enter a URL address in this box and press Return to start the transfer. In 1.x, this box was simply to inform you of your location. It could not be used for entering URLs. The URL box can be toggled on and off in the Options menu (Show URL). See Figure 3-36.

*Note: The other method of entering URLs is found under the File menu as Open URL... (or Command+U).*

URL: http://www.ncsa.uiuc.edu/SDG/Software/Mosaic/NCSAMosaicHome.html

Figure 3-36: *The URL box.*

## What Is a URL?

Uniform Resource Locator (or URL) is a system that the World Wide Web uses to standardize the addresses of various types of Internet services. Each type of service, HTTP (HTML document transfer), Gopher, FTP, USENET News, etc., has a constant type of URL address that Web browsing software can read. Although these addresses are lengthy, and look intimidating at first, they become easier to read as you get more familiar with their structure.

### Anatomy of a URL

A URL usually consists of three parts: the method of access, the location of the computer where the desired files or services are available and the path to those files.

- The Access Method (or Protocol)
  This is the first part of the address, usually separated from the rest of the address by a colon and a double slash (://). This tells Mosaic what type of service it will be connecting to.

- Location of Computer Site
  The name of the computer site where the service or file is located (usually found directly after the double slash).

- File Path Name
  The specific name and location of the file being sought. This can be anything from the name of a file directory to the full path to the file itself. Sometimes a URL consists of only the first two parts and there will be no specified file (i.e., http://www.wired.com).

| Access Method | Type of Access |
|---|---|
| http | World Wide Web server file (Hypertext Transport Protocol) |
| file | Files on your local system or on anonymous FTP server |
| ftp | Remote file transfers (File Transport Protocol) |
| gopher | Connects you to a Gopher server |
| news | USENET Newsgroups (reading only) |

Table 3-5: *Common types of URLs.*

## Reading URLs

The basic structure of a URL looks like this:

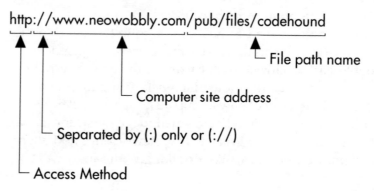

Here are some examples of URLs and what they mean:

**http://www.wired.com**
**http://www.wired.com/Etext/2.07/features/patents.extras.html**
The first http URL takes you to the home page of the WWW server at wired.com, an electronic magazine stand run by *Wired* magazine. The second URL will take you directly to an electronic text version of an article on patents that appeared in *Wired* 2.07.

**gopher://well.com**
**gopher://gopher.well.sf.ca.us/00/Publications/authors/Sterling/fsf/**
**buckymania**
The first URL accesses the Gopher site at the WELL BBS. The second URL goes directly to an article called "Buckymania" written by Bruce Sterling. This article is located in the authors section of the Publications directory.

**ftp://ftp.eff.org**
**ftp://ftp.eff.org/pub/EFF/about.eff**
The first URL will take you to the EFF's (Electronic Frontier Foundation) FTP site. The second one accesses an introduction to the EFF located in the EFF section of the Pub directory.

**news:rec.music.industrial**
**news:2upl68$3b9@jimbo.muppet.bt.co.uk**
The URL form for accessing a USENET Newsgroup through Mosaic is different than the other forms discussed above. Here it's just news: (with no double slash) followed by the name of the newsgroup. In this example, we have accessed the industrial music group found within the rec (recreation) category of newsgroups. The second example shows the full path name to an article located in rec.music.industrial. To find out more about using Mosaic to read newsgroups and alternative newsreaders, see Chapter 4, "Web Walking With Mosaic."

## Voice Navigation

Mosaic 2.x comes with speech recognition capabilities. For this feature to work, you'll need to have Apple's Speech Recognition extension properly installed in your System folder. Table 3-5 lists the speakable commands that Mosaic will recognize and what the resultant actions are.

| Voice Command | Action |
|---|---|
| Mosaic | Brings Mosaic to the front (if deactivated). |
| Bring Mosaic to front | (same effect as above) |
| Computer quit Mosaic | Quits out of Mosaic. |
| Mosaic go back | Goes back to the previous page (same as pressing the Back button). |
| Mosaic previous document | (same effect as above) |
| Mosaic go forward | Goes forward to the next page (same as pressing the Forward button. |
| Mosaic next document | (same effect as above) |
| Mosaic go home | Returns to the home page. |
| Mosaic page up | Advances the current document up one page. |
| Mosaic page down | Advances the current document down one page. |
| Mosaic page home | Advances the current document to the top of page. |
| Mosaic page end | Advances the current document to the bottom of page. |

Table 3-5: *Speakable commands in Mosaic 2.x.*

To voice activate hotlinks, read the link as it is displayed on the screen. If the link is a picture, the picture is named "Picture <NUMBER>"

(i.e., PICTURE 62). Mosaic will handle up to six words in a link name. If the link contains more than six words, the rest are ignored. If the link contains more than three words, the last three are optional. The first three words are required (if there are that many in the link name).

## Moving On

If you've read through this chapter, congratulations! You now know most of what you'll need to be a Web walker extraordinaire. You at least know your way around all of Mosaic's most commonly used features. These are the tools you'll need to venture deep into the Web. Three features, Helper Applications, Tag Styles and Hotlinks, are especially important. Be sure you

- Have all the Helper Applications you'll need to view graphics and movies and to hear audio clips (see page 46).
- Learn enough about how Tag Styles work in Mosaic to control the look of your Web documents (see page 52).
- Know how the Hotlists feature works (see page 59).

In Chapter 4, we'll finally move beyond the confines of the Mosaic program and into the rich fabric of the Web itself. We'll look at how to find your way around and how to access the various forms of hypermedia that are floating around. We'll also explore the many Internet services you can access with Mosaic and how you can stay abreast of the latest news and information about Mosaic and the Web.

Now that we have the basic technical aspects out of the way and we're ready to roll, let's go for a stroll through the Web to see what kind of trouble we can get ourselves into. Cyberspace beckons.

**Lost in the tangle of hypertext?** History in hypermedia is very important. Studies done early in the development of hypertext found that people had a hard time staying "connected" to their thought process if they got lost in a hyper-tangle of information. Encouraging self-exploration is a great benefit to hypertext/hypermedia, but that needs to be balanced with a sense of logical organization. Being able to see where you've been and to move back to previous branching off points is very important. In Mosaic, the History window, the Back, Forward and Home buttons, and the hotlink colors help you keep track of where you've been and the documents you've browsed along the way.

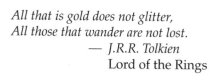

# WEB WALKING WITH MOSAIC

*All that is gold does not glitter,*
*All those that wander are not lost.*
— *J.R.R. Tolkien*
Lord of the Rings

Jumping into cyberspace has always been an exciting experience for me. Even my first login, as frustrating as it was, gave me the Net bug. I had acquired a funky 300 baud modem and was itchin' to see what it could do. It came with no documentation and I really had no clue how to install or use it. Sticking the circuit board inside my Apple IIe, I did get it up and running—sort of. I tried logging into some local BBSes and the newly formed (now rather famous) Whole Earth 'Lectronic Link (the WELL) in Sausalito, California. It was like hearing a radio message from a ship lost at sea. There was so much line noise in among the text that I could barely make out what was going on. But I was still fascinated. I immediately got a sense that there were all these tiny ports of call in some vast electronic ocean. There were people "in" there... talking to each other...having fun...exchanging information...building something unique. After several more noisy modem sessions, I gave up in disgust. I would have to wait for a real modem. I held out for about six months, until I couldn't take it any longer. I had to get back online to see what I was missing. I went out and bought a new computer and a 2400 baud modem, dialed up the WELL and have hardly been offline a day since. That was 1987—several lifetimes in computer years.

Mosaic is not your parents' Internet. Until recently, the language of the Internet (and its ancestors) was rather harsh and intimidating to learn. To navigate through the Net, you needed persistence and a head for second guessing how machines "think." And, on top of that, everything had to be communicated in plain text. It was far from what you would call a user-friendly environment. Information services like CompuServe, Delphi and America Online have tried to make things easier, with login software and graphic interfaces, but they are not the Internet. The quality of the information and virtual community they offer is not nearly as impressive as the Net at large. Mosaic and programs like it will change all that. They are bringing the ease of an online service to the information riches of the Internet. And, with the addition of hypermedia and an easy-to-use document creation system, they are moving far beyond the media desert of the "old" Internet and into an uncharted oasis.

Web walking feels different than other types of Internet experiences. The beehive of activity taking place there is visible regardless of how you're logged in, but a screenful of text, however brilliant, is very different from a hyperlinked web of texts with accompanying multimedia. When I log onto the UNIX-based WELL BBS, I run through a text list of conferences, and then through topics within those conferences. I come to the end of a topic, and if I want to say something, I post a response. Then I move on to the next conference down the line. It's all very list-like—from top to bottom.

On the Web, there is this feeling of being potentially everywhere at once, or at least everywhere that's hyperlinked to the site you're on and everywhere that those subsequent sites are linked to, and so on. It feels vastly interconnective in a fashion that makes "web" certainly an apt description. Being in the Web, with its graphical user interface and all of its hypermedia offerings, is an immense thrill to a Net old-timer like myself. Having been involved in hypermedia, specifically HyperCard, for many years, the Web is like a HyperCard stack that spans the globe. It even has pop-up QuickTime movies, graphics windows and a Home button!

But enough hyping Mosaic for a moment. Let's stroll onto the Web and I'll show you a bit of what I'm talking about.

## A Web Session

The first place Mosaic takes you upon launching is the home page. Since I don't want to add to the high volume of data traffic that the NCSA site is getting (the default home page in Mosaic), I've pointed the program toward my own home page. See Figure 4-1. This page lives on my hard drive and is not actually on the World Wide Web.

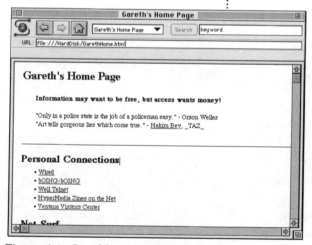

Figure 4-1: *Gareth's Home Page.*

Once my home page is loaded into Mosaic, I can go anywhere on the Web from there. The home page I've made has hotlinks to the Web sites I frequent. Later on in this chapter, I'll show you how to create your own home page.

### Internet Connections List

From here (our home page), let's check out Scott Yanoff's Special Internet Connections List. It's a great source of links to a diverse range of Internet offerings. I press Command+U to pop up the URL box and then type in the location (**http://info.cern.ch/hypertext/DataSources/Yanoff.html**). Pressing the Return key starts the connection. Once connected, Scott's List appears in the Mosaic window. It includes lots of hotlinks to telnet addresses, gopher sites, finger sites and, of course, more Web sites.

The range of topics and interests include agriculture, ham radio, games, philosophy, aviation, careers and family issues. Since I'm in the mood for something more recreational and for sites I can show off to you, let's take a hotlink to the Internet Mall to see if it's gotten any better since the last time I was there.

## The Internet Mall

Nope. It still has a rather vacant, gloomy feeling to it, like a new real-world mall that's already opened a couple of stores and all the rest are curtained with signs that promise: Coming Soon! Everyone's trying to make pretend that there's excitement in the air, but it's not heartfelt. The Grand Opening hasn't happened yet. The Internet Mall feels exactly like that. It's organized by floors: First Floor: Media, Second Floor: Personal Items, Third Floor: Computer Hardware and Software, Fourth Floor: Services telnet books.com. There are currently only a few items on each "floor." Not finding much of interest here, I decide to try the link to the Future Fantasy Bookstore.
**http://www.kei.com/internet-mall.html**

## Future Fantasy Bookstore

This virtual bookshop has a real-world counterpart in Palo Alto, California. On the Web, they offer their book catalog (in Mosaic 2.x you can type in search information and fill out order forms), new book listings, back issues of their newsletters and some fantasy art. In the new book area, you can click on the name of the book and view its cover art or click on the author's name to see all the books that Future Fantasy carries by that author. Trouble is, I don't like fantasy. I came, attracted to the "Future" part of their name, but I don't see much in the way of sci-fi titles. I *do* see a link to the Science Fiction Resource Guide at Rutgers University. After goofing around here for a while, looking at some full-color scans of book covers and searching on a few authors, I jump across the Web in search of the sci-fi guide. **http://www.commerce.digital.com/palo-alto/FutureFantasy/home.html)**

## Science Fiction Resource Guide

This place turns out to be the mother lode. The Guide contains a staggering amount of information on science fiction literature, film, TV and criticism. The first thing I see is a hotlink to "A Short History of the Internet" by my WELL buddy, sci-fi writer and cyberpundit Bruce Sterling. (Nice essay, BTW. I hope people will read it. If you do choose to read this, be sure to return to the Science Fiction Resource Guide to keep up with our tour.) Scrolling through the home page of the Guide I pass dozens of links to essays, reviews, articles, interviews, even whole books (e.g., Sterling's *Hacker Crackdown*). There are long lists of subject bibliographies, sci-fi film and TV show synopses, links to sci-fi critical journals, conventions and awards—and if that's not enough, there are links to all the other sci-fi archives in the Web! **ftp://gandalf.rutgers.edu/pub/sfl/sf-resource.guide.html**

If I were on my own, I would probably spend the rest of the night scrambling along these interconnected threads, reading some of the interviews and other material available here (a FAQ for *Brazil*, my favorite movie, and a three-part FAQ on the *Alien* films). But since I'm trying to show off the Web to you tonight, I'll move on. Before I leave, I press Command+D to automatically add this page to my current hotlist. (See "Creating Your First Hotlist" on page 60 in Chapter 3 for more information on hotlists.) I notice a link to the Best of the Net page (of which the Science Fiction Resource Guide is a worthy recipient). Let's go and see who else was so honored.

## Best of the Net

A nice big blue logo welcomes you to the Best of the Net sponsored by *GNN Magazine*.

**http://src.doc.ic.ac.uk/gnn/meta/internet/feat/best.html**

The award winners are listed and described, with hotlinks to each of them. The 1994 winners are (envelope please):

Figure 4-2: *GNN's Best of the Net logo.*

### ArtServe

ArtServe is an art history database consisting of 2,800 images of prints, largely from the 15th century to the end of the 19th century, and 2,500 images of mainly classical architecture and architectural sculpture from around the Mediterranean. From here, you can also link to the Canberra School of Art.

**http://rubens.anu.edu.au/**

### The Currency Converter

The Currency Converter is a script that converts currency from one denomination to another. Choose the country that interests you and view its approximate rate of exchange with other countries.

**http://www.ora.com/cgi-bin/ora/currency**

### Edupage Newsletter

Educom is a non-profit consortium of higher education institutions seeking to transform education through information technologies. The Edupage Newsletter, published three times a week, summarizes printed news coverage of interest to all Net citizens.

**http://www.educom.edu/**

### International Teletimes

*International Teletimes* is a general-interest magazine published online by sixteen-year-old Ian Wojtowicz. According to Ian, "Teletimes seeks

to present informed opinion and observation drawn from the experience of living in a particular place."
**http://www.wimsey.com/teletimes.root/teletimes_home_page.html**

## Internet Underground Music Archive

Billed as the "Net's first free hi-fi music archive." The Archive also seeks to promote obscure and unsigned bands.
**http://sunsite.unc.edu/ianc/**

## New Zealand Information

Everything you always wanted to know about New Zealand—and then some. Geography, language, food, culture and wildlife.
**http://www.cs.cmu.edu:8001/Web/People/mjw/NZ/MainPage.html**

## The Paleontology Server

An interactive natural history museum on the Net. Learn about phylogeny, the "Tree of Life," or examine photographs of great white sharks off the California coast.
**coast.http://ucmp1.berkeley.edu/welcome.html**

## Science Fiction Resource Guide

"More information on Science Fiction than any one person can comfortably keep track of." I'll say!
**ftp://gandalf.rutgers.edu/pub/sfl/sf-resource.guide.html**

## Taxing Times

Taxing Times is a repository of tax forms, including many electronic IRS publications.
**http://www.scubed.com:8001/tax/tax.html**

## U.S. Census Information Server

Here you can get financial data on state and local governments as well as schools. The Census Bureau Art Gallery has a display of posters used to promote participation in the census.
**http://www.census.gov/**

## Hypertext USENET FAQs

A hypertext database of FAQs (Frequently Asked Questions) available on the Internet.
**http://www.cis.ohio-state.edu/hypertext/faq/usenet/FAQ-List.html**

## HOT TIP

You don't have to go to all the places hotlinked on a Web document to add them to your hotlists. For any item that looks interesting, you simply have to move the finger cursor over its hotlink. This will make the Status Messages area display the link's URL (assuming you have "Show Status Messages" selected in the Options menu). Select Add Doc in the Hotlist Items window and type in the name of the document and its URL in the appropriate boxes. Click OK. The document will now be added to your current hotlist.

## Xerox PARC MapViewer

MapViewer is an application that dynamically renders a map based on user input. Click on a region and MapViewer zooms in on it. You can also use a geographic name server to locate a particular location by name.
**http://pubweb.parc.xerox.com/map**

This looks like an exciting list of Web locations (well, I might skip the tax and census sites). First let's take a look at ArtServe. But before we do, we'll add this document (Best of the Net) to our hotlist by pressing Command+D. That way, we can come back and check out all of these documents at our leisure.

## ArtServe

This site offers both an art and architecture collection and some art

Figure 4-3: *Heinrich Aldegrever (1502-1555?), Intemperance.*

tours. You can view the databases alphabetically, with or without thumbnail images, or you can search the databases on keywords (Mosaic 2.x only). I decide to browse through the print collection with the inline images turned off. Pressing on the image I want to see, a small thumbnail reproduction pops up. If I then want to view the entire image, I press on the thumbnail to begin downloading a larger version. When the download is complete, Mosaic opens up JPEGView (assuming you have the JPEGView Helper Application on your hard drive) and begins decompressing the image (see Figure 4-3). When I'm done viewing, I quit JPEGView and am returned to the art database. After some more browsing and downloading, I decide to leave. But again, before I do, I'll add this site to a hotlist. I plan to come back and take a tour of the architecture section. As a graphic designer, this could prove to be a significant resource for me. Because I perceive this site as a valuable work-related resource, I add it to my "Art and Design" hotlist instead of my general hotlist (Hotlist1). From here I check out the Xerox PARC Map Viewer and then call it a night. Because the Map Viewer is not hotlinked on this document, I need to return to the Best of the Net page to take the link from there. I click on the History list and slide up to highlight that location. From the Best of the Net page, I click on Xerox PARC's hyperlink.

## Xerox PARC MapViewer

The MapViewer proves to be very easy to use. First, to find out what your map coordinates are, you have to take a hyperlink to the U.S. Geographic Name Server. By typing in the city and state in Mosaic's Search box, you find the map coordinates you want to view. The coordinates are hotlinked. By clicking on them, you're taken back to the MapViewer and your location is plotted on the map. I typed in my hometown, Arlington, Virginia. Here's what my map looks like. See Figure 4-4.

After about two hours online, I'm bushed. I press Command+Q to quit Mosaic and then make sure my SLIP has been disconnected. The main thing I'm excited about from this little jaunt is the Science Fiction Resource Guide. I plan to return there as soon as I have some free time (after this book is finished!). The Best of the Net had other offerings I want to check out as well. An electronic magazine called *International Teletimes* edited by a sixteen-year-old kid seemed enticing. Toto, I don't think we're in Kansas anymore.

Now that we've had a full-blown trip through the Web and have tried some of its hypermedia offerings, let's take a closer look at how these media (hotlinks, inline images, graphics and movies) work. In the previous chapter we looked at the features contained within the Mosaic program. In this chapter, we'll look at the contents of the Web itself and how to bring its awesome resources to your desktop using Mosaic.

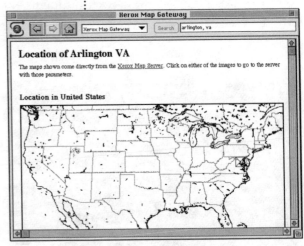

Figure 4-4: *The Xerox PARC MapViewer.*

## ⟲ HOT TIP ──·──·──·──·──·──·──·──

If you want to keep a record of your entire Web session, create a new hotlist (see "Creating Your First Hotlist" on page 60 in Chapter 3) and name it something like "Web Session 6/20/94," or whatever is appropriate for you. Now, every time you go to a new page, press Command+D to add that page to your session hotlist. You'll end up with a record of all the places you visited during your session. After you quit the session, your record will be saved (unlike the regular History feature).

──·──·──·──·──·──·──·──

## Hypermedia in Mosaic

As we discussed in Chapter 1, hypermedia is the marriage of hypertext and multimedia (sounds, graphics, movies). While the real lifeblood of the World Wide Web is still text, its multimedia aspects are important and will become more so as the Web expands, as connections become faster and as browsers like Mosaic become more sophisticated. While onlookers may find the QuickTime movies and the pop-up images of a SLIP/PPP-connected Mosaic pure novelty, the visionary knows that he or she is looking at the future. It may appear as though we're getting all excited about silent films in an age of breathtaking color cinematography, but it's the potential of the medium that's so alluring. The sense of anticipation and a spirit of cooperation is everywhere in cyberspace, with lots of people working alone or in small groups, chipping in to wire the planet for a hypermedia feed.

Right now things *are* rather crude. A SLIP/PPP-connected machine running Mosaic can be a tortoise-like media delivery system. Compressed images do well—some are downright stunning—but they take several minutes to download. Movie downloads are even slower, and the quality is often poor. Hopefully, multimedia technology will see some breakthroughs in the near future (QuickTime 2?) and Net-based hypermedia will get a much needed upgrade. Lots of sites are now using forms, user-input boxes, digital signatures, pictures with multiple hotlinks in them and other advances in Web interactivity. Next year's Web will be a far cry from this year's Web. Or so we hope.

The main forms of media currently available in Mosaic are

- Inline Image—color and black-and-white graphics that appear as part of the Web document.

- GIF, TIFF and JPEG images—color and black-and-white graphics that are transferred to your Mac and are opened up by an external viewing application.

- QuickTime movies—moving images in the QuickTime format that are transferred to your Mac and played on an external movie player.

- MPEG movie—moving images in the MPEG format that are transferred to your Mac and played on an external movie player.

- Audio—music, spoken words and sounds that are transferred to your Mac and played on an external audio player.

## Inline Images

Next to text, the most common element in a Web document is the inline image. These are graphics that can either be transferred with the rest of the page (if Auto-Load Images has been turned on), or marked by an icon that gives the option of loading (or not loading) the image after the page has been downloaded.

Inline Image icon

Inline images might be confusing at first because a similar icon is used to hotlink larger graphics, sounds, movies and even other Web documents. Besides the arrow over the icon, the difference between an inline image and a piece of hotlinked media is that inline images all

Hotlinking icon

load to the screen when Auto-Load Images is selected. They are resi-
dent to the current document. Hotlinked media will not load automatically. You must click on the icon to retrieve the image, movie or sound,
or to go to the page hotlinked via the inline icon.

On a directly connected Internet machine, you can choose to keep the
Auto-Load Images option turned on. This way, you'll instantly see the
whole Web page as its creator intended it, as soon as it's been transferred. On a SLIP/PPP-connected machine, having all the inlines
transferred when you connect to a site can be very time consuming,
especially if you have no idea beforehand how many images are stored
on the page. For this type of connection, the best procedure is to

1. Keep Auto-Load Images turned off in the Options menu.

2. When you get to a site and you've read through the text, click on the
inline image and hotlink icons that interest you. Sometimes you will be
given clues in the text as to what's behind these icons, sometimes you
won't. If you are unsure about the size of a hotlinked media item
(indicated by the inline icon with an arrow on top) and you don't want
to bother loading anything that's too large, you can choose Use Header
Mode from the Options window (in Mosaic 2.x only) and click on the
hotlinked name of the item (*not* the icon) to get info about its size. The
Use Header Mode does not work for regular inline images or on
hotlinked item icons themselves.

Really thoughtful Web page makers will put a small caption under
the inline icon telling you what the item is and how large it is. Also,
images are sometimes repeated on the same page. Since they are
cached, they don't take any extra time to download.

Here are the various inline image icons encountered in Mosaic.

| Inline Icon | What It Means |
|---|---|
| | Basic inline image icon with image not loaded. |
| | Basic inline image loaded. |
| | Inline image with size and type specified. |
| | Hotlink with inline image not loaded. (If you don't want to load the inline image before taking the link, you can press on the arrow above the icon.) |
| | Hotlink with inline image loaded (by clicking on this image, the user will be taken to a text link or a sound, image or movie). |
| | Inline image load has failed (try choosing Reload from the File menu). |

Table 4-1: *Inline image icons.*

Inline image icon

Picture preview

Speaker icon

There are three phases to accessing something indicated by an inline image icon with an arrow on top. Assuming you have Auto-Load Images turned off, you would follow these steps:

1. Click on the inline image icon with arrow.

2. A small graphic or preview image will be loaded.

3. If you still want to access the full file, you would click anywhere inside the preview image. The larger image, movie or sound will be transferred and displayed. If this icon is being used to indicate a link to another Web document, by clicking on the inline image you will be taken to the new page. In the above example, clicking on the preview image icon will bring you to a small image of Vice President Gore. Click this image and a full-screen JPEG version of the same image will be transferred.

*Note: If you don't wish to view the inline image before going to the linked item, you don't have to. Click on the blue arrow above the inline image icon and you will move directly to the hotlinked item.*

4. If the inline image icon is a link to an audio file, when you load the inline, you will usually get some type of speaker icon. By clicking on this icon, the audio file will be downloaded. When the transfer is complete, Mosaic will open up the audio Helper Application and immediately play the clip—unless you've altered Mosaic's "Launch Immediately" default setting in the Helper Configuration window (see Chapter 3).

As Mosaic loads files to your machine, the Status Indicator changes to reflect what type of file is being loaded. To see what those indicators are, see Table 4-2.

| Indicator | What It Means |
|---|---|
| | Mosaic at rest. Nothing is being transferred. |
| | Mosaic is connecting to a computer site. |
| | Text is being loaded. |
| | A GIF, JPEG or TIFF file is being loaded. |
| | An MPEG or QuickTime movie is being loaded. |
| | An audio file is being loaded |
| | A compressed data file is being transferred. |

Table 4-2: *Status Indicator icons.*

**HOT TIP**

If you want to go directly to a piece of hotlinked media without having the hotlink inline image load first, you can double-click on the image icon.

As long as the little yellow lights are visible on the Status Indicator, the download is still in progress. Sometimes it will temporarily stop moving and the cursor with change from the Mac watch icon to the arrow cursor. The transfer is not complete until the lights are "turned off" on the Status Indicator and the cursor has returned to the finger icon.

## GIF, JPEG & TIFF Images

While Mosaic has embedded within it the resources to present small images, larger, more complex images are best handled by one of the external viewing programs such as JPEGView and GIFConverter. When you click on an inline image or a text hotlink that is attached to a larger graphic, the Status Indicator switches to the graphic icon and the transfer begins. Once an image has been transferred, it's stored in Mosaic's Temp Directory (as specified in Preferences), and the external viewer assigned by Mosaic to handle that file type is launched. For GIF and JPEG images, JPEGView is the default application. For TIFF images, GIFConverter is recommended (see Chapter 3 for full details on how to select other viewers). The viewer application begins to process the image and displays it as soon as it's decompressed.

After viewing the image, you can either choose to close the external viewer (which will keep the application launched but in the background) or you can quit and return to Mosaic. Mosaic automatically reopens the viewer the next time it's needed.

If you want Mosaic to always give you the option of saving an image to disk, follow the instructions in Chapter 3 on "Configuring Helper Applications." When the window pops up giving you the check box option "Ask User for File Name," check the box. From now on, when that image type is transferred, Mosaic gives you the option of naming it and saving it. Obviously you don't have to name and save the ones you're not interested in.

## QuickTime & MPEG Movies

If you encounter any movies online, you can transfer and view them if you have the appropriate players installed (see Chapter 3). It's a good idea to have both the QuickTime and MPEG players installed since Web documents will not always specify what type of format their movies are in. You also want to be careful to check out how big the files are before you transfer them. Some movies are megabytes in size. Luckily most Web documents do tell you the file sizes (see Figure 4-5). If they don't, choose the "Use Header Mode" from the Options menu and click on the movie hotlink to see its size (Mosaic 2.x only).

QuickTime movies work fine (or at least OK) on all QuickTime-compatible Macs, while MPEG movies do better on higher-end machines like Centris and Quadras. If you are unsatisfied with the quality of MPEG movies on your machine, you can get better quality out of them by converting them to QuickTime.

1. Click on the hotlink or inline image of the MPEG movie to transfer it to your screen.

2. Once the transfer is complete and the MPEG movie player pops up, choose Save As... in the File menu.

---

```
Files: Size (bytes) - Date - Name (sorted)
 60502 - 22 Mar 09:16 - 3d-mri-brain.mpg
369069 - 22 Mar 09:16 - 3d-mri-head.mpg
740175 - 22 Mar 09:11 - BigE_Anim.mpg
339528 - 22 Mar 09:23 - DebbieHarry.mpg
730973 - 22 Mar 09:37 - IMloopy.mpg
873335 - 29 Mar 08:14 - andrew.mpg
```

Figure 4-5: *Example of how movies should be listed in a Web document. Some lists give no indication of movie format or size.*

Figure 4-6: *QuickTime viewer.*

3. Select the QuickTime format and click on Save.

4. A box of compression settings appears. Ignore it (unless you know what you're doing) and choose OK.

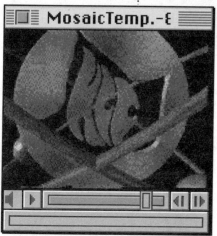

Figure 4-7: *MPEG viewer.*

5. The MPEG player starts saving the movie frame-by-frame to QuickTime format. The converted MPEG movie is now on your hard drive.

6. To view, you'll need to launch your QuickTime movie player.

Figures 4-6 and 4-7 show typical QuickTime and MPEG movie viewers. Your mileage may vary depending on which viewers you're using. The ones pictured here are BijouPlay (QuickTime) and Sparkle (MPEG). The extra bar under the Sparkle viewer is a status bar that shows the program's progress as it's converting a movie from one format to the other.

## HOT TIP

Media files, especially movies and sounds, can be very large and take up a lot of (temporary) space on your hard disk. Keep an eye on your disk space if you're downloading a lot of big files during a Mosaic session. If you start to worry about how much file space you're eating up, you can choose "Remove Temp Files" from the Options menu and the files will be deleted.

If you want Mosaic to always give you the option of saving your movies to disk, follow the instructions in Chapter 3 on "Configuring Helper Applications." When the window pops up giving you the check box option "Ask User for File Name," check the box. From now on, when the movie type you have done this to is transferred, Mosaic gives you the option of naming it and saving it. Obviously you don't have to name and save the ones you're not interested in.

The way MPEG handles frame-to-frame compression is fascinating. Since most video consists of a series of objects moving in the foreground and relative static in the background, MPEG only transmits the motion of the foreground objects, rather than retransmitting both the foreground and the background over and over again. MPEG uses a form of pattern recognition to decide which pixels are part of moving objects (and therefore transmittable) and which are not.

## Audio

Mosaic lets you access spoken words, music and other forms of audio. These are transferred in the same manner as images and movies. Since audio of any significant length can take up a lot of disk space (and take forever to download), you'll want to know the size of the audio file before you request it. Some Web pages will tell you the size, others won't. The Use Header Mode option can tell you the file size before you download it. Figure 4-8 shows the control window of a typical audio playback/record application. The application shown is SoundMachine, a full-featured sound tool that can also be used to record sounds to attach to your Web documents.

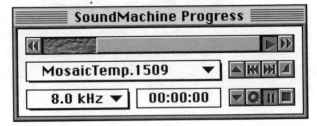

Figure 4-8: *SoundMachine, a typical audio record/ playback application for the Mac.*

## ✏ HOT TIP

Since Mosaic keeps temporary items until you quit the application, if after you've quit out of a Helper Application you decide that you do want to keep the image, movie or sound, you still can. Find the temporary file on your hard disk (it will be labeled "Mosaic Temp" followed by a number). This file will be located in the "Temp Directory" specified in Mosaic's Preferences area. Click on the file icon's name field and rename it whatever you want. Move it to the folder where you want it stored and return to Mosaic. You must do this while Mosaic is still running. Otherwise, when you Quit the program, all the temporary files will be removed. If you have a bunch of Mosaic Temp files in the directory and you're not sure which one you want to save, move them all out of the folder and go through them after you quit your Mosaic session to find the one(s) you wish to keep. You must then manually trash the rest.

## Using Mosaic as an Internet "Front End"

One of the things that distinguishes Mosaic from other Web browsers is that it's not only a hypermedia browsing tool—it can also be used to access regular Internet services such as FTP, telnet, Gopher and WAIS. You can even read USENET Newsgroups from within Mosaic. In the following section, we'll run through each type of service and describe how you can best take advantage of it using Mosaic.

### FTP

File transfer, the ability to freely move documents and programs from computers all over the Internet and into your home computer, is one of the big advantages of Net connectivity. Using Gopher, Web search engines and other tools, you can find information on just about anything. If I hear about a new piece of free software, an electronic magazine or something else that's recently floated into the Net, I can usually find it and download it in a matter of minutes. File Transfer Protocol (FTP) is the main standard used on the Internet for transferring files from one computer to another. While FTP-ing is not difficult in any of its forms (see Chapter 2), it is especially easy with Mosaic. To access an FTP site you'll need the FTP server's URL. This address will be in the form ftp://site/filepath (if any). See Table 4-3 for more information on URL forms for Internet services. Many FTP sites are hotlinked, so all you have to do is click on the link and you will be transported either to the site or directly to the file itself. Once you're at the site and have found the document you're looking for (usually stored in a document hierarchy not unfamiliar to Mac users), all you need to do is

1. Click on the name of the file you want to FTP.

2. A typical Save File dialog box pops up asking you to name and direct the file to the appropriate place on your hard drive. Mosaic then transfers the file the same way it would a graphic, movie or sound. The Status Indicator will change to indicate what type of file it is transferring (in this case usually the compressed data indicator).

Compressed data indicator

3. When the transfer is complete, Mosaic automatically unstuffs the file and places it on your hard drive.

That's all there is to it. See Table 4-4 for descriptions of many of the file types found on an FTP site and how Mosaic handles them.

*Note: Clicking on the file folder or document icon within an FTP directory will do nothing (if icons are visible). These are non-functional internal images that are used to indicate the directory hierarchy and the various file types. You must click on the file name, not the icon, to begin the transfer.*

| Service Name | URL Form | Type of Service | Notes |
|---|---|---|---|
| World Wide Web | http://site[/filepath] | Hypermedia documents | Using HTTP (Hypertext Transport Protocol) for connecting to HTTP servers (Web sites) |
| FTP | ftp://site[/filepath] | File transfer | Used for transferring files to your computer |
| Gopher | gopher://site[/filepath] | Menu-driven info. browser | Used for browsing and transferring files to your computer |
| Telnet | telnet://site | Remote login | Use to connect to another machine on the Internet |
| News | news:newsgroupname | Reading USENET news | You need to enter the name of your local news server in the Preferences box to access newsgroups |
| Email | (not applicable) | Electronic mail | To send mail while in Mosaic, use NCSA Telnet to log into a host that offers mail or use a mail program like Eudora |
| WAIS | waisindex wais://site/database | Searchable databases | Search on keywords for text documents (mostly) that can then be transferred to your computer |
| Finger | http://www.cs.indiana.edu/finger/ | Get information about users | In Mosaic, you need to go through a hostname/username gateway to access the UNIX finger command. |

Table 4-3: *Internet services and how to connect to them through Mosaic.*

*Note: On the Web, many of these documents are hotlinked so you will not have to enter a URL. You simply click on the name of the service (or document on the service) to connect to it.*

| Icon | Extension | File Type | Downloading Notes |
|------|-----------|-----------|-------------------|
| | (none) | Directory | Cannot be downloaded. The folder icon is simply used to indicate a directory on the FTP server. |
| | .sit | File compressed with StuffIt. | Mosaic will transfer and automatically decompress with StuffIt Expander. |
| | .hqx | File compressed w/BinHex | Mosaic will transfer and automatically decompress with StuffIt Expander. |
| | .txt | Plain Text | Will be transferred to Mosaic's document window. |
| | .mpg | MPEG movie format | Mosaic will transfer file and launch external MPEG player. |
| | .mov | QuickTime movie format | Mosaic will transfer file and launch external QuickTime player. |
| | .au | Audio file format | Mosaic will transfer file and launch external audio application. |
| | .jpeg | JPEG image format | Mosaic will transfer file and launch external JPEG viewer. |
| | .gif | GIF image format | Mosaic will transfer file and launch external GIF viewer. |
| | .tiff | TIFF image format | Mosaic will transfer file and launch external TIFF viewer. |

Table 4-4: *Common file types found on FTP and Gopher sites using Mosaic.*

*Notes:*

*1. "automatically unstuff" assumes you have the appropriate Helper Applications on your hard drive. For the file types above, Mosaic has defaulted the following applications: StuffIt Expander (for the various compressed files), Sparkle (for MPEG Movies), SimplePlayer (for QuickTime), SoundMachine (for audio), JPEGView (for GIF and JPEG files) and GIFConverter (for TIFF files). See Chapter 3 for instructions on how to locate and add Helper Applications.*

*2. The icons pictured above will not appear at every FTP and Gopher site. Some sites will not have icons at all and you'll have to look at the extension (.mpg, .hqx, .au, etc.) to figure out what type of file it is.*

*3. You may also encounter files with the extensions .cpt (Compact Pro) and .sea (Self-Extracting Archive). These will also be transferred by Mosaic and passed off to StuffIt Expander for automatic unpacking.*

## Gopher

The Internet Gophers ("go for") provide information search and re-trieval on computer systems throughout the world. Connecting to a Gopher server using Mosaic works exactly the same as connecting to an FTP site. You browse through a hierarchy of directories and files until you find the file you wish to transfer. When found, you simply click on its name to begin the transfer. You can access a Gopher site either by clicking on a hotlink that's pointing to a Gopher or by typing a Gopher URL into the URL box. The form would be gopher://site/filepath (if any). Table 4-4 shows many of the file types you might encounter in Gopherspace.

## Telnet

Telnet is a computer terminal protocol that lets you log on to other computers on the Internet. For instance, I use the telnet command to log onto the WELL in Sausalito, California. To do this, I log on to my UNIX account at a local Net site and then give the telnet command to "open well.com." I am instantly transported to the WELL's front door where I can log in and go about my business. In Mosaic, there is no ability to send email or to log in to another computer remotely. The solution to this is an excellent piece of freeware from NCSA called NCSA Telnet. It works the same way as Helper Applications. If you come to an Internet resource that requires you to log in to a remote machine to access it, the telnet address will either be typed out or hotlinked. If typed, you'll need to enter its URL in the URL box (in the form telnet://site) and choose Open. If it's hotlinked, all you do is click on the link. If you have NCSA Telnet installed on your machine, Mosaic automatically launches it and makes the connection. That's all there is to it. You don't need to do anything to configure NCSA Telnet. Just load it onto your hard drive. The program does offer a full range of features and has extensive documentation available as a separate download. You can FTP NCSA Telnet from ftp.ncsa.uiuc.edu, or it's usually hotlinked to the MacMosaic Web page at NCSA. See Figure 4-9.

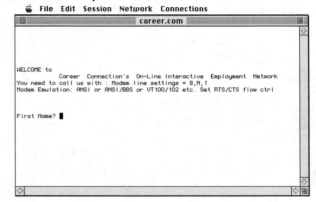

Figure 4-9: *A remote login from Mosaic using NCSA Telnet.*

HOT TIP ⎯ . ⎯ . ⎯ . ⎯ . ⎯ . ⎯ . ⎯ . ⎯ . ⎯ . ⎯

Don't forget you can use the Apple Scrapbook or Note Pad to cut and paste URLs you find while in Mosaic or while using other Internet services. That way, by saving them electronically and not writing them down, you remove the risk of copying them incorrectly.

⎯ . ⎯ . ⎯ . ⎯ . ⎯ . ⎯ . ⎯ . ⎯ . ⎯ . ⎯ . ⎯ . ⎯

## USENET Newsgroups

USENET Newsgroups are one of the biggest attractions on the Internet. These are discussion groups covering every conceivable subject. The discussions are often erudite, funny, feisty and bizarre. They are like global town meetings divided into special interest groups of staggering variety.

While Mosaic allows you to read these USENET groups, you can't join in on the conversations or have much control over the news feed. If, after listening in for a while, you get interested in posting messages, it's recommended that you download a freeware newsreader program and use that instead of Mosaic. That way, you'll not only be able to read the discussions, you'll be able to roll up your sleeves and dive right into them.

Reading newsgroups with Mosaic is a cinch. If you remember, in Chapter 3 we entered the address for a "newshost" in the Preferences window. This is the address of the local Internet provider that carries USENET news. Mosaic accesses this local server when you want to read your groups. To access a newsgroup, you need to know its name. Many of the Internet books in the bibliography include lists of all the major newsgroups. Once you know the group's name, say rec.arts.tv, you need to put it in a form that Mosaic understands. This would be news:rec.arts.tv. All you do is type **news:newsgroupname** in the URL box and click Open. In a few seconds, you'll be looking at the current discussion on that topic—in this case, the latest offerings on the *other* monitor in your house.

The titles of the twenty most recent postings (called "articles") to a newsgroup appear on your screen in a hotlinked list. To read one of the messages, just click on the title and the full article will be displayed. There is

Figure 4-10: *A USENET newsgroup in Mosaic.*

always a hotlinked item at the top of the window called Earlier articles. By clicking on this, you can access the previous twenty postings. See Figure 4-10.

## WAIS

WAIS (pronounced "ways") is a text search and retrieval system similar to FTP and Gopher. An acronym for Wide-Area Information Server, WAIS gives you the ability to search databases of mostly text-based documents by using keyword queries. Similar to Gopher, you don't have to know anything about what type of database is being accessed or where it's located. WAIS deals with all this for you. Unlike Gopher, you can't browse the databases; you can only keep trying keyword combinations and hope for a match. WAIS databases cover everything from agriculture to social sciences. The easiest way to plug into the WAIS system is to go to **http://info.cern.ch/hypertext/ Products/WAIS/Sources/Overview.html**. There you'll find a master index of WAIS databases.

## Finger

Finger is a utility that lets you look up information about users on UNIX systems. Most of the time a user's Finger file consists of their login name, their real name, the last time they accessed their account and if they have any unread mail. There is also an area in the Finger file to show a "plan," which can be a bio or anything else the user wants other people to see. Many UNIX system administrators don't make the Finger files available over the Internet without the express permission of the users of their system. Some people use Finger files as a way of broadcasting information to the Net. There are Finger files with baseball scores, quotes of the day, California

**Newsgroup Readers**  Mosaic, for all its virtues, only gives you a peek at USENET Newsgroups. You can read groups, but you can't respond to them. If you're interested in participating in these global discussion groups, you need to use a newsreader program. There are a number of good newsreaders that are freely available over the Net. Nuntius is a popular one that's easy to install, configure and use. It, and other newsgroup readers, are available from the following FTP sites:

| FTP Site | Directory Path |
|---|---|
| bitsy.mit.edu | /pub/mac/news/ nuntius |
| mac.archive.umich.edu | /mac/util/comm/ usenet |

earthquake information and other news and trivia. These public information Finger files are traded over the Net like other cool sites, newsgroups and mailing lists. Some Net artists put ASCII-based art into their files. In Mosaic, you can access Finger files by going through a gateway that accesses Finger. The gateway address is **http://cs.indiana.edu/finger/gateway**. Here you can read more information about Finger files and the WWW gateway to them. You can also search on a Finger file from anywhere within the Web by using the URL **http://www.cs.indiana.edu/finger/hostname/ username**. For instance, to view a Finger file of late-breaking NASA news, type **http://www.cs.indiana.edu/ finger/space.mit.edu/nasanews**. See Figure 4-11.

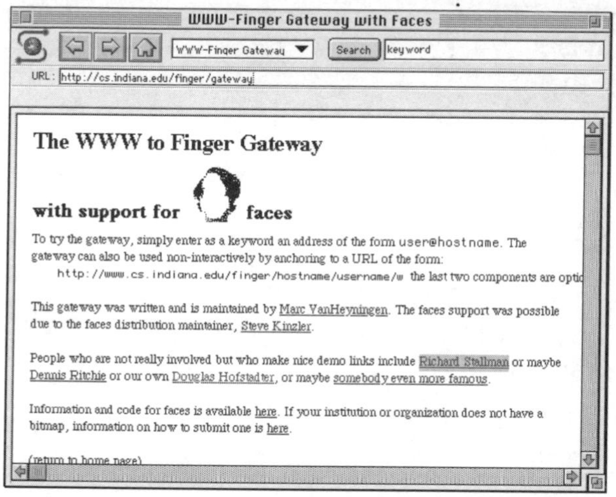

Figure 4-11: *The Finger Gateway.*

## HTML ASAP: Making Your Own Web Documents

Making your own Web documents isn't rocket science—in fact, it isn't hard at all. If you can use a word processor and are familiar with fonts and style changes (bold, italic, underline), you can create HTML documents. HyperText Markup Language is simply a method for marking text in such a way that it looks and behaves the way you want it to when it's viewed in a Web browser. The marking codes may look arcane at first, but once you get the hang of them, you'll be confident in moving on to more sophisticated document construction.

Let's get started by making a simple home page. All you'll need is a text editor and a little patience.

## Format Containers

Browsers that read HTML (like Mosaic) use only the formatting tags you enter when formatting text. All spaces, tabs and indentations you put in the original text are ignored when your HTML document is displayed in Mosaic. So, to make things look the way you want them, you've got to use the appropriate formatting tags.

For the most part, HTML formatting tags surround (or contain) the text you want to format. For instance, if you want something to appear in boldfaced type, you need to tag the text with bold codes, like this:

<B>The Web is Wide, Wild and Wonderful</B>

The first three characters, <B>, mark the beginning of the HTML formatting. The "B" character indicates boldface. The "Less Than" (<) and "Greater Than" (>) symbols set the tags off from the actual text. The message "The Web is Wide, Wild and Wonderful" is the text that is being marked for presentation in boldface. Finally, the line ends with the code </B>. This marks the end of the area that is tagged as bold. All HTML tags end with the same </code> form.

The important thing to remember is that HTML considers most formatting codes to be "containers" that hold data to be formatted (in this case the sentence "The Web is Wide, Wild and Wonderful"). The neat thing about this concept is that you can place containers within containers. This is called "nesting" and can be used for things like applying two attributes to one object. For example:

<I><B>The Web is Wide, Wild and Wonderful</B></I>

Now our sentence "The Web is Wide, Wild and Wonderful" will appear as both bold and italic, because it is contained within bold and italic formatting containers.

Believe it or not, those are the basics. Armed with the knowledge that WWW browsers only look at formatting codes to decide how to show your text, and that these codes are containers that can be nested, you're now ready to dig deeper—constructing your own home page, complete with images and hyperlinks.

## The HTML Style Tags

The foundation of any HTML document is its many formatting codes, or "tags." Table 4-5 lists the basic tags and what part of an HTML document they effect.

## Winning Web Page Design

With the increasing number of Net users with Web access, and thanks to the ease with which HTML documents can be created, there's starting to be a glut of really bad page designs. Terrible text layout, unnecessary use of large images and audio clips, and content of questionable merit are elements in far too many documents. As in many situations where there's a spirit of open access and an "anyone can participate" attitude, mediocrity can quickly take over. Here are a few design suggestions to keep in mind when creating Web documents.

- "K.I.S.S." is an acronym commonly used in graphic arts. It stands for "Keep it simple, stupid!" This and all basic rules of graphic design should apply to Web pages. You are publishing something that thousands of people may see. *Add* to their visual field, don't clutter it with trash. Try to keep the number of stylistic elements to a minimum and work the flow of the document so it has as much impact as possible. An old graphic arts trick is to squint when you're looking at a page of design. By fuzzing your vision a bit, you can see the elements of a page as interacting objects rather than their specific content. Do this on your documents until the elements are balanced (or unbalanced in a pleasing way).

| Begin Code | End Code | Format | Description |
|---|---|---|---|
| <TITLE> | </TITLE> | Title | What your document is called on the Web. |
| <H1> | </H1> | Headers | Headings differentiate between parts of your document. |
| <IMG SRC=""> | Not applicable | Image | This causes an inline image to be displayed. |
| <A HREF=""> | </A> | Link | A way of pointing at a different Web document, a media clip, etc. |
| <P> | Not applicable | Paragraph | A paragraph of text. Unlike the other formatting commands, you only have to put the <P> tag at the beginning of the paragraph. |
| <BR> | Not applicable | Line break | Same as a hard return. |
| <B> | </B> | Bold | Shows text in bold face type. |
| <I> | </I> | Italic | Shows text in italic type. |
| <U> | </U> | Underline | Underlines a word or phrase. |
| <A NAME=""> | </A> | Internal Link | Links to other parts of the same document. |
| <OL> | </OL> | Ordered (numbered) List | Causes a list of items to appear with identifying numbers next to each element. |
| <UL> | </UL> | Unordered (bullet) List | Causes lists to appear with bullets, asterisks or + signs next to each list item, depending on the browser. |

Table 4-5: *Basic HTML formatting tags.*

- Keep in mind that different types of browsers will be used to view your documents. While lots of graphics and jazzy color elements might look great on your browser, someone using a text-based browser (such as Lynx) might just see a confused mess.

- White space can be a good thing. Learn how and when to use it to your advantage. Set things off for emphasis by surrounding them with white space.

- Try to "chunk" information into logical units. Use common sense and an eye toward logical organization when you're laying out your documents. It is best to let the material unfold in levels, rather than having everything appear at once.

- Integrate your links into the material. Don't put "Click here!" off by itself with no point of reference. Your links should go where they make the most sense, ideally in context. If you do put them off by themselves, say what they are: "More information on widgets."

- Check your links! It's a nuisance to find a document that has links that don't go anywhere. Before you post your documents, make sure everything works.

- Be literate. Again, this is as much a publishing environment as anything else. Use a spell checker and read over everything before you post it. One writer's tip: Read out loud what you've written. If it sounds good spoken, chances are it will read well on the page.

- Sign *all* of your documents. People like to know who wrote Web documents, and ideally, how to contact them. Don't just sign the "front" page of a document series. Sometimes people will come in the back or side doors to your documents (if they have a URL to a page that's not the first). If you don't label these secondary pages, no one will know whose handiwork they are.

- Give as much information as possible about the size and content of inline images and hotlinked media. You can label inline images with a caption (57K image) or hotlinked media with a written description: "1.2Mb performance video in MPEG format." If a media item is really huge, it should have an even more emphatic message: "CAUTION: This QuickTime movie is 2.7Mb in size!" (Remember, people don't read instructions. You have to shout sometimes.)

- Limit your use of inline images. Try to find small, high-impact images, and overall, use images sparingly. Think in terms of the different types of users who will be accessing your pages. Some may have fancy Silicon Graphics workstations connected to T5 lines, but others will be putting along at 14,400 baud. Try to create pages that will communicate and satisfy at all levels. It's a challenge, but it can be done.

- Don't be afraid to break any of these rules if you've got a good reason for doing so.

## Building Your Home Page

Your most basic home page would consist of a title, a header or two and some text. At this point, we won't worry about links, images and sounds. To begin,

1. Open a new document in your favorite text editor or word processing program.

2. Decide on a title for your home page. "My Home Page" is probably as good a place to start as any. Since the title of your page should appear as the first line in your HTML document, type **<TITLE>** to indicate you are about to enter the title of your page.

3. Next, type in the name of your home page and then **</TITLE>** to indicate the end of the title. Your document should look like this:

<TITLE>My Home Page</TITLE>

4. Let's put a header at the top of the page. There are six levels of header tags in HTML, with each level down a slightly smaller typeface. Since this is your top header, and you want to make it big, you should use Header level 1.

5. Type **<H1>** to indicate the beginning of your header and then type the actual header. Something like "Welcome to My Home Page." Finally, type **</H1>** to indicate the end of the header. So far, your home page HTML document should look like this:

<TITLE>My Home Page</TITLE>
<H1>Welcome to My Home Page</H1>

6. Now, add some text or a blurb about yourself. Since this information might be several lines long, you'll want to use the paragraph HTML tag so that it formats correctly. Type a **<P>** tag, hit enter to get to the next line and type some stuff about your home page, like this:

<P>
This is my first home page. It will be my jumping off point into the rest of the Web. Hello cyberspace!

*Note: Remember, Mosaic doesn't care how many blank lines you use, or how many spaces you indent your paragraph, or where you put the line breaks. Mosaic is only concerned with the way the document is tagged. So, if you do want the lines to break at a specific point, such as in a poem, you need to put a <BR> code at the end of the line where the break should occur. This is like hitting a hard return at the end of each line in a word processor. If you do this, no matter how big or small the Mosaic window is, it will go to the next line when it encounters the <BR> code.*

At this point, your home page HTML document should look like this:

```
<TITLE>My Home Page</TITLE>
<H1>Welcome to My Home Page</H1>
<P>
```
This is my first home page. It will be my jumping off point into the rest of the Web. Hello cyberspace!

You have now constructed a working home page! A little dull maybe, but it *is* an HTML document and will function quite nicely as a home page until you want to get more elaborate. Let's go look at it in Mosaic.

7. Save your document as a text file in the Mosaic folder. Call it whatever you like (e.g., "home.html"), but make sure it ends in .html.

8. Launch Mosaic and select Open Local from the File menu. From the Open Local dialog box, find your text file and click the Open button. Your home page should now load and be visible within the Mosaic document window. How does it look?

9. To permanently make this your home page, pull down the Options menu and select Use This URL for Home. You've done it! Now when Mosaic starts up, you'll go directly to this home page on your local hard drive rather than having to wait for it to connect to NCSA. If you want to go to NCSA once you're in Mosaic, you can still get there by choosing its name from the Navigate menu.

## Adding Some Pizzazz

Face it, a home page like this is pretty boring. If you've been doing any Web walking, you know that the WWW is just bursting at the seams with graphics, sounds and hotlinks. In fact, if you came upon a home page like the one you've just constructed, you'd probably keep right on walkin'. The great thing about HTML is that adding all the media files is as easy as formatting them!

To add a link to a picture on your hard drive,

1. Find a suitable picture. If you have a scanner, you can scan something in—a picture of yourself, for instance. Or, how about a piece of computer art? It doesn't matter what it is, as long as it's in GIF format (and not too huge). If you have a picture in another format—TIFF, JPEG or PICT—use GIFConverter (or something similar) to convert the picture to GIF.

2. Put the picture in the same folder as your home page and name it <name.gif>, with "name" being whatever you choose.

3. Open your home page HTML document in your text editor. To insert a link to your picture, enter a special tag that tells Mosaic where to look for the picture when it opens your home page. Type **<IMG SRC="name.gif">**

You need to type this in the place in your document where you want the picture to appear. For example, if you want the picture to appear below the first header in your home page, you would add the line like this:

```
<TITLE>My Home Page</TITLE>
<H1>Welcome to my Home Page</H1>
<IMG SRC="name.gif">
<P>
```

This is my first home page. It will be my jumping off point into the rest of the Web. Hello cyberspace!

4. Save your HTML document and open up Mosaic. If you haven't quit Mosaic since you last admired your home page, you'll have to select Reload from the File menu.

If you look up at the Status Indicator as your home page is being reloaded, you'll see that the icon changes to the graphic indicator. That's your picture being loaded.

If all goes well, and you have the Auto-Load Images option on, your picture will appear when your page does. If you have the Auto-Load option turned off, you'll see an inline image icon where your picture is "stored." If for some reason your image doesn't load (if it's not a GIF or you didn't type the name in correctly) you'll see an x-ed out inline image icon indicating that the image load has failed.

Now that you have a picture on the page, how about adding some sounds?

1. First, record your sound with SoundMachine (one of your Helper Applications) and save it as an .au sound file in the same directory as your home page. Say you record a greeting, you could call it "greeting.au".

Since Mosaic won't auto-load sounds like it does images, you'll have to put in a link to your sound. A link can be anything: a word, a sentence or an inline image. In this case, we'll just use a word as our link.

2. Construct the link to your sound by typing the tag into the place where you want the link to appear on your home page. For example,

<A HREF=

This tag tells Mosaic you want to link to whatever comes after the = .

3. Next, type the name of your file in quotes.

**<A HREF="greeting.au"**

4. To make a link show up in your home page, you need to type in the description of what you are linking to. First, type >, the beginning of the container for the link's name. Next, type in the name of the link as you want it to appear on your home page. In this case, let's use "Click here for greeting!" Your line should now look like this:

<A HREF="greeting.au">Click here for greeting!

5. To end the line, type **</A>** to mark the end of your tag. Your final sound link tag looks like this:

&lt;A HREF="greeting.au"&gt;Click here for greeting!&lt;/A&gt;

6. Save your home page HTML document, open Mosaic and watch your home page load. You should see your new greeting link appear. Click on it to hear the audio.

## Links to the Outside World

You now have a snazzy little multimedia home page! But something important is still missing. You have no way of getting onto the Web. You need to add some hotlinks so you can easily take off from this home page to global ports of call.

The basic format of any link is the familiar URL. If you were asleep during the URL discussion in Chapter 3, you should go back there now and brush up on what a URL is and how it works.

Before you add any links to your home page, you'll want to add a new header to indicate that this is a hotlinks section of the document.

1. Open your home page in your text editor. Go to the end of the document. Since this header is below the first header in terms of the layout priority of the document, you'll want to use a Header level 2 this time. Type something like

**&lt;H2&gt;Links to the Outside World&lt;/H2&gt;**

2. Now you can add a few handy links. A good one is the NCSA What's New Page. By checking this page frequently, you can keep track of all the latest Web happenings and announcements.

3. To construct a link to this page, you'll use a format similar to the one we used to link sound. The sound link was to a file on your own machine. Since here you want to connect to a file (the NCSA What's New Page) on another server, a URL is needed to make the connection.

Below your second header, type **<A HREF="HTTP://
www.ncsa.uiuc.edu/SDG/Software/Mosaic/Docs/whats-new.html"**

This line tells Mosaic to go to the NCSA WWW server
(www.ncsa.uiuc.edu), skip to the /SDG/Software/Mosaic/Docs/
directory and grab the file "whats-new.html."

4. Just like the sound file, you need to have some way of indicating on
the home page that there's a link. Add a link description similar to the
one for sound. Type **>What's New on the Web</A>** at the end of the
URL line. The whole line should now look like this:

<A HREF="HTTP://www.ncsa.uiuc.edu/SDG/Software/Mosaic/
Docs/whats-new.html">What's New on the Web</A>

When this line loads into Mosaic, you'll see "What's New on the
Web" underlined.

5. How about adding another link? Sometimes you want to search for
something on the Web but have no idea where to find it. Something
called a Web search engine keeps an index of all the contents of the
WWW and lets you search on it by keywords. When it finds a match,
you get a list of those matched items, presented as hotlinks. These
search engines are like robot librarians with a collection that spans the
globe. An excellent and highly recommended search engine is called
the WebCrawler. To add a link to it, go to the next line in your document and type **<A HREF="HTTP://www.biotech.washington.edu/
WebCrawler/WebQuery.html">WebCrawler Search</A>**

When this appears in your Mosiac document, all you'll have to do is
click on the words "WebCrawler Search" and you'll be instantly transported to the WebCrawler's home at the University of Washington.

Now that you've got two links in a row, you've got a list! Well, at
least *you* think it's a list. Mosaic still thinks that it's two links right next
to each other. Remember, Mosaic doesn't know diddly about text

formatting! To put the two links into list form for Mosaic, you have to attach HTML tags.

There are two major types of lists: numbered and unnumbered. Numbered lists have numbers appearing at the beginning of each unique list item. Unnumbered lists have a bullet in front of each item. They both work the same way, so it's up to you which one to use. Here's how to add a list-format container:

1. Go to the point just above the first item (NCSA What's New Page) and hit Return to insert a blank line. If you want your list to be numbered, type **<OL>** for "ordered list." If you want an unnumbered list, type **<UL>**.

2. Next to each link, type **<LI>** to indicate that the link is a list *item*.

3. Close the container by going to the line right beneath the last link and typing **</OL>** if you have a numbered list and **</UL>** if you have an unnumbered list.

4. Save your document, open it up in Mosaic and gloat— you have now constructed a full-featured home page!

You can add as many links as you like by either adding them in as we've outlined above, or by cutting and pasting them from other HTML documents.

## Your First HTML Document

Your home page HTML document should look like this (see Figure 4-12):

<TITLE>My Home Page</TITLE>
<H1>Welcome to my Home Page</H1>
<IMG SRC="name.gif">
<A HREF="greeting.au">Click here for greeting!</A>
<P>

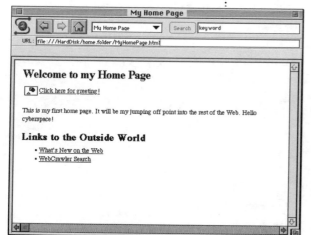

Figure 4-12: *My Home Page.*

This is my first home page. It will be my jumping off point into the rest of the Web. Hello cyberspace!
<H2>Links to the Outside World</H2>
<UL>
<LI><A HREF="HTTP://www.ncsa.uiuc.edu/SDG/Software/ Mosaic/Docs/whats-new.html">What's New on the Web</A>
<LI><A HREF="HTTP://www.biotech.washington.edu/WebCrawler/ WebQuery.html">WebCrawler Search</A>
</UL>

Now that you've gotten your first taste of HTML document making, you may want to delve deeper into how it's done. Why not use this as an opportunity to ask your robot librarian for some advice. Go to the WebCrawler and do a search on "HTML" (or maybe more specific things like "HTML Primer" or "HTML Style Guide").

## HOT TIP

A great way to learn how to create HTML documents is to look at other people's. You can mimic, copy, cut, paste and add to/change what they've done. Use the Load to Disk option to save a Web document to your hard drive. Open it up in a word processing program and monkey around with it to your heart's content. Then, choose Open Local from the Mosaic File menu, find the document and double-click on it. If it didn't turn out the way you planned, you can open it up again in the word processor while you're still running Mosaic. Make further changes, save the document, and then choose Reload from Mosaic's File menu. The altered document will appear inside the Mosaic document window. Using this tinkering and experimenting back and forth, you can learn a lot about how HTML making works.

## Staying on the Crest of the Wave

Things move quickly in cyberspace. Just when you think you have a handle on what's going on—when you think you're in the vanguard—you discover a whole new corner of the Net that you knew nothing about. Mosaic and WWW are like that. It seems as though the Web has just now caught the attention of many Net citizens. They are often shocked to learn that the Web has been around for years and that it's as large as it is. Now that you're a full-fledged Web walker, you can use the impressive resources of the Web to stay on top of its development. Listed below are many of the key documents, Web sites and USENET newsgroups that cover the late-breaking news and announcements concerning WWW and Mosaic.

### FAQs & Other Reading Material

An amazing collection of Web information packed into a single document. The *comp.info-systems.www FAQ* covers just about everything you need to know about starting out on the Web, the basics of HTML, a description of relevant terms and lots more.

**comp.infosystems.www FAQ**
**http://sunsite.unc.edu/boutell/faq/www_faq.html**

### WWW Primer

The *WWW Primer* is a friendly introductory guide to the Web. Much more accessible than a lot of the FAQs and a lot better written then most "primers."

**http://www.vuw.ac.nz/who/Nathan.Torkington/ideas/www-primer.html**

---

**Top 10 Signs Your WWW Home Page Is *Not Cool***

10. Hotlist is only lukewarm.

9. Links to your page keep using the adjective "fetid."

8. Disney wants to buy the rights to use it in Mighty Ducks III.

7. On Adam Curry's list of neat home pages.

6. WWW Worm got bored and left.

5. Condemned by the housing authority.

4. Word "cool" is in the title.

3. Nancy Kerrigan says it's the corniest page she's ever seen.

2. Geek Code replaced by Geek C++ Code.

And the number one sign your home page is not cool...

1. Access log shows tons of visits by Al Gore.

—Found on the Web

---

### Entering the World-Wide Web: A Guide to Cyberspace

A thick treatise by Kevin Hughes on the World Wide Web, with history, basic concepts, places to visit, a hypermedia timeline and a glossary of terms.

**http://www.eit.com/**

## Information Sites

### Mosaic Information Site

A great starting point for seeking any type of Net/Web-related information and help. Lots of links fan out from here.

**http://www.ncsa.uiuc.edu/SDG/Software/Mosaic/MetaIndex.html**

### WWW Information Site

The WWW Information Site graciously provides a link breakdown of WWW-related information. Users, developers, service providers and Web page authors will all find plenty of interest here. And, because it's all hyperlinked, each of the links connects to even more interesting Net points. A good place to start if you have a specific subject area you want to explore.

**http://www.bsdi.com/sever/doc/wes-info**

## Newsgroups

### news.answers

*The* repository for FAQ files from across the Internet. A huge body of information is accessible here. Before you ask, get the FAQs! All FAQ files that are posted to this newsgroup are archived at **ftp:// rtfm.mit.edu/** or **ftp://ftp.uu.net/usenet/news.answers/**

They are also available in HTML format at **http://www.cis.ohio-state.edu/hypertext/faq/usenet/FAQ-List.html**

### comp.infosystems.announce

This newsgroup for the announcement of new information systems has also become the de facto place to announce new Web pages and sites. The University of Rochester has created a Web document announcing all the new pages announcements posted to this group. You can access the Rochester document at **http://www.cs.rochester.edu/users/grads/ferguson/announce/**

It's a good idea to add this address to one of your hotlink lists.

### comp.infosystems.www.users

For discussions of browsing software, new user questions and general news, information and assistance.

### comp.infosystems.www.providers

If you're interesting in setting up and administering a WWW server, this is the place to find out more about it.

### comp.infosystems.www.misc

This group is set up to discuss everything not covered in the other WWW newsgroups. The future of the Web, protocols and standards have been recent topics of interest.

### comp.infosystems.www (defunct)

Comp.infosystems.www was the original group created for discussing WWW. It has now been subdivided into the groups listed above. Many sites that carry USENET news still include it, but it will soon dissolve in favor of the other comp.infosytems.www.* groups.

### comp.sys.mac.comm

Covers computer telecommunications for the Macintosh. Contains information on all sorts of Mac telecom products and services, including Mosaic for Mac and other WWW browsers. Also contains discussions on setting up and maintaining SLIP/PPP connections and other aspects of plugging your Mac into the Internet.

### alt.hypertext

Discussions of hypertext, both in and out of the World Wide Web. People often announce their Web hypertext projects here. The FAQ file for this newsgroup can be found at **gopher://ftp.cs.berkeley.edu**

### alt.etext

Discussions on all forms of electronic texts. Not strictly related to hypertext or the WWW, but often includes postings on where to find electronic texts on the Web and how to set up your own e-texts in Webspace.

## Other Applications to Ease Your Net.Life

The Helper Application scheme used in Mosaic is brilliant. As has been said earlier, it frees Mosaic up to do what it does best and it gives you, the user, the flexibility of choosing what types of applications and which specific applications you want Mosaic to use for media presentations and file decompression. Even NCSA Telnet, while not considered an "official" Helper Application, works like one within Mosaic (see section on telnet above). But, alas, Mosaic doesn't think of everything. Most importantly, it doesn't handle email or full newsgroup participation. Here are a number of excellent freeware programs that you can use to fill in the gaps left by Mosaic.

### Eudora

Even if Mosaic does get email support in a future upgrade, chances are you'll still need an extra program to read mail. Eudora is one of the best Macintosh email programs around, offering scriptability, Finger, aliases, filtering, sorting and lots of other sophisticated features. Eudora is easy to find on the Net and easy to set up.

## NewsWatcher

NewsWatcher is a dedicated USENET newsgroup reading program. It lets you set up lists of newsgroups you want to subscribe to, loading only the lists you want to view. You read the news by clicking on the names of the articles as they appear in the newsgroup window. NewsWatcher actually uses several "Helper Apps" of its own. With the addition of uuUndo, you can download and decode "binary" files posted to picture-, sound- and program-related newsgroups.

## Nuntius

Like NewsWatcher, Nuntius lets you configure and read USENET news via an intuitive Mac interface. You can maintain lists of newsgroups that you can read by pointing and clicking, and you can even decode binary files from within the program. Why not download both of these newsreaders and see which one you're most comfortable with. Some people swear by NewsWatcher, others by Nuntius.

## TurboGopher

There may be times when you don't want to fire up Mosaic just to look up some information. For those quick and dirty info grabs, you might want to use TurboGopher. TurboGopher is a Gopher client that makes use of standard Mac features. Gopher directories appear as folder icons and individual Gopher files are shown as document icons. Because Gophers don't really have much, if any, multimedia capability, TurboGopher tends to run much faster than Mosaic, especially on lower-end Macs. It's definitely no substitute for the hyperlinked, multimedia Web, but TurboGopher is still great for a quick burrow through the Net.

## Anarchie

Similar to Fetch (see Chapter 2), Anarchie is an FTP client for the Mac. Unlike Fetch, however, Anarchie adds several useful features. First, it includes an integrated Archie file lookup client, so you can use it to search for hard-to-find files. It comes preconfigured with many of the global Mac FTP sites and directories, allowing you to jump right in with just a click of the mouse. Also, it features variable-size windows that can even be enlarged to full-screen size—a far cry from Fetch's little mutt-size windows.

## Hotlist2HTML

This little application performs the elegant task of translating Mosaic's binary-formatted hotlists into text files readable as HTML documents. This is useful if you want to share your sizzlin' hotlists with someone who's using a WWW browser on another type of computer. Tip: It's very easy to run your hotlist through this program and then edit the document, add some information about yourself and voilà—instant home page!

## BBEdit & HTMLExtensions

BBEdit is a programmer's text editor available in both a feature-rich commercial version and the good-enough-for-all-but-superhackers shareware version. It translates and saves text files in Mac, PC and UNIX formats so that documents you write in BBEdit can be read by people using other machines. HTMLExtensions are plug-in modules providing BBEdit with the ability to create HTML documents just by highlighting text and selecting HTML tags from a menu. Very useful!

**Tales From Hyperspace**  Members of the academic community have been keenly interested in hypertext since the1960s. Within the realm of progressive literature, it's seen as a writing technology ideally suited for communicating the fragmented and multifaceted nature of postmodern life. So far, most of the experiments in "hyperlit" have been done by individual authors, in HyperCard or other hypertext programs, and distributed on disk as electronic books. John Schull and Charles Deemer have a different idea. They want to grow the world's first collaborative Web novel. Called *Stories from Downtown Anywhere*, this hypertext work will incorporate many voices and many levels of talent. Anyone on the Net is free to submit work for consideration by the book's editors. Interlocking smaller stories are hyperlinked to create a larger fictional universe. If you read a story thread and see something you want to develop, a character, a physical space or anything else that strikes your fancy, you email your suggestions to the project's editors for approval. Once your contributions have been accepted, they are hotlinked into the story. The novel is also interactive, with at →

least two choices in narrative direction available within each story fragment.

The URL for the project is http://www.awa.com/stories/

From here, you can link to all the existing parts of the story (so far there are only a few) or find out information on how to contribute your own tales.

### HTML Editor

This is the premiere WYSIWYG (what you see is what you get—pronounced wizzy-wig) HTML editor for the Mac. Using this editor to tag text in an HTML document, the results show up looking like they would inside of Mosaic. While this editor is not necessary for creating your own home pages, it is helpful for more visually oriented Web page makers.

*Note: Most, if not all, of the programs listed above are available from **ftp://sumex-aim.stanford.eud/info-mac/comm/tcp/** or from the Ventana Visitors Center (**ftp://vmedia.com/pub/Mac**)*

## Moving On

Hopefully you've now had enough time online to understand how the Web works and what Mosaic has to offer. If you haven't tried all of its features, take some time to go back through this chapter, focusing especially on browsing the Best of the Net award-winning sites and trying out the various Internet services that Mosaic can access. Doing this will put both you and Mosaic through your paces (and in Mosaic's case, make sure that it's properly configured and that all the Helper Applications are installed).

Chapter 5 is a directory of Web sites, covering everything from online libraries and art galleries to electronic magazines and recreation centers. This is not a exhaustive catalog, but thanks to the beauty of hypermedia, all these sites are connected to dozens more, which are connected to still more, and on and on. There are enough access points here to take you deep into the fabric of the Web. In fact there's enough connections to keep you busy for years. So pack a lunch, lace up your power walking shoes and scamper onto the first available Web link that strikes your fancy.

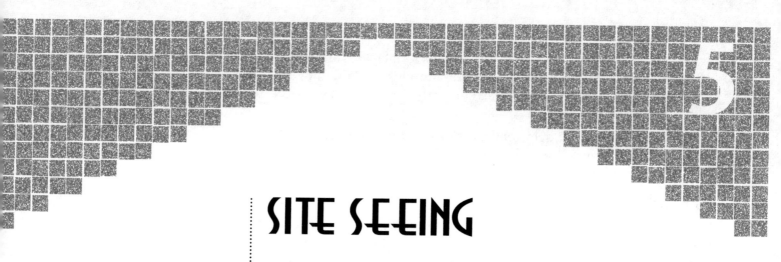

# SITE SEEING

*"Would you tell me, please, which way I ought to go from here?"*
*"That depends a good deal on where you want to get to," said the Cat.*
*— Lewis Carroll*
     *Alice in Wonderland*

**O**ne of the more amazing things about a good hypertext environment like the World Wide Web is how quickly you can worm your way through it, going from "cool" links to "hot" ones. In the Web walk we went on in Chapter 4, it only took a few links to travel from a very general document with lots of material of little interest to several Web pages full of material I wanted to read (and to hotlink).

The resources covered in this chapter are far from exhaustive. There are too many sites and this book is far too modest an effort to record even a smidgen of the documents available. But the Web sites outlined below are junctions in a complex pattern of connected threads. One can lead to hundreds. If you were to act like a Web spider and follow all the links that are attached to these pages, and all their subsequent links...well...it would be a fascinating journey to say the least.

The site listings in this chapter are divided into three sections:

- General Net Resources, a veritable university on, and about, the Internet.

- Robot Librarians, indexes, search engines, databases and robots that can act as your electronic guides through the labyrinth of the Net. Learn how to use them properly and all of cyberspace will be your oyster.

- Cool Sites to Visit, some of the best, most useful and just plain weird sites and sounds available on the Web. Divided by category.

## General Net Resources

It's been said that the best guide to the Internet is the Internet itself. You can put this adage to the test by going to the Virtual University represented by the listings below. Between them, they provide every level of detail you might want on Internet history, software tools, techniques and thoughts on future Net innovations. For Net vets, checking in with these sites is a good way to keep up with the latest Net technologies.

### The Guide to Network Resource Tools

A hypertext introduction to all of the major Internet networking tools (WAIS, Gopher, NetNews, X.500, Hytelnet, telnet, etc.). Covers where to find them, how to use them and where to go for more information.
**http://www.earn.net/gnrt/notice.html**

### *Internaut*

The online cousin to *The Online User's Encyclopedia* (Addison-Wesley, 1994), a comprehensive guide to computer networks from TCP/IP to FidoNet, BITNET, UUCP, WWIVNet and RIME. Online resources include back issues of *Internaut*, with overview articles, how-to's and letters to the editor. Also contains information about the encyclopedia and where to get it.
**http://www.zilker.net/users/internaut/index.html**

## Internet Resource Guides

A clearinghouse of subject-oriented resource guides available on the Internet. This Web page has links to the Gopher site at the University of Michigan Library where the guides are accessible. They are divided into sections: Humanities, Social Sciences, Sciences and Multiple Subject Coverage. You can also search the full text of the collection. A number of HTML versions of some of these guides are also available.
**http://http2.sils.umich.edu/~lou/chhome.html**

### HOT TIP

Having a problem connecting to some of the sites listed? You may be trying to access a popular site during its peak traffic hours. Don't despair—if at first you don't connect, keep at it.

Internet Tools

## The Internet Tools List

A large catalog describing the various tools that can be used on the Internet for information retrieval, computer-mediated communication and other services. A number of the tool listings are hotlinked to FTP sites so the software being discussed can be easily downloaded.
**ftp://ftp.rpi.edu/pub/communications/internet-tools.html**

## The Web Overview at CERN

Web documents maintained by the creators of the World Wide Web. A broad overview of the Web, organized by subject, listing Web servers by country and by type of services offered.
**http://info.cern.ch/hypertext/WWW/LineMode/Defaults/default.html**

## Robot Librarians

You're in a hurry, you need information on the Shoemaker-Levy 9 comet for a paper that's due tomorrow. Or you want to know about all the Web sites that cover film and video. Whatever resources you may be tracking down in the vast halls of the world's virtual libraries, you could always use a librarian to help you. The sites listed in this section are either "self-service" information sources or they come with automated information "librarians" that will tirelessly race through the Web to find the resources you're after.

## Babel Computer Terms

A glossary of computer-oriented abbreviations and acronyms. It's a shame that there are no definitions included; some of these abbreviations are quite obscure. Just knowing that POPF stands for Pop Flags isn't enough. What on earth are Pop Flags? Still a source of worthwhile clues to the many obscure references found in computer and telecom documents and discussions.
**ftp://ftp.temple.edu/pub/info/help-net**

## Britannica Online

The *Encyclopedia Britannica*'s online test site. Still in the beta test phase, but there are articles you can browse. Lets you search on keywords. Supports both form searches (Mosaic 2.x) and list searches (Mosaic 1.x). This will be a paid subscription service when it is up and running.
**http://www.eb.com/**

## CERN WWW Virtual Library

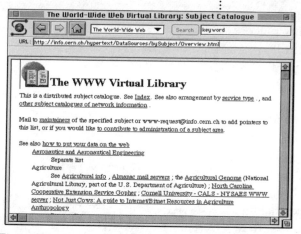

Figure 5-1: *The World-Wide Web Virtual Library.*

This library is the granddaddy of all Web hotlink pages, having its humble origins in the days when the Web was text-only. The Virtual Library's "by subject" approach to Web indexing is a helpful way to begin your Web travels. **http://info.cern.ch/hypertext/DataSources/bySubject/Overview.html**

## Dictionaries

While it might seem odd that a site in Germany is the main link point to a bunch of English dictionaries, this service is undeniably useful. Here, you can gain access to a number of literary, grammatical and lexigraphical reference books. Includes *American English, Webster's, Roget's Thesaurus, The Oxford Dictionary of Familiar Quotations* and an online computer dictionary. Plus many more. **http://math-www.uni-paderborn.de/HTML/Dictionaries.html**

## Gopher Jewels

Gopher Jewels is a moderated list service of interesting finds from Gopher sites. It covers dozens of categories on everything from agriculture and forestry to fun to library sciences. The interface is attractive and easy to use. **http://galaxy.einet.net/GJ/index.html**

## Index to Multimedia Sources

If graphics are what you crave, if plain text doesn't cut it for you or if you just want some nifty stuff to impress that friend who's looking over your shoulder, than the Index to Multimedia Sources is the place to go. It doesn't include a link to *every* multimedia resource, but it comes close. Here you can find links to media archives, multimedia software, conference announcements, media-related companies and much more.

**http://cui_www.unige.ch/OSG/MultimediaInfo**

## FAQ List

The FAQ List is a major repository of Net wisdom, alphabetized by subject. Perhaps the most info-dense node in cyberspace, the FAQ List lets you browse Frequently Asked Question files by pointing and clicking. From information on Apple II emulators to tasteless jokes and creative cooking. You can sound like an expert in no time; just read the FAQs.

**http://www.cis.ohio-state.edu/hypertext/faq/usenet/FAQ-List.html**

## Nexor List of Web Robots

This Web Robots page links you to most of the better "robots," programs that automatically hunt the Web and index the results of their searches. Having a Web robot is like having your own data-sniffing hound dog!

**http://web.nexor.co.uk/mak/doc/robots/active.html**

## Internet Connections List

Scott Yanoff's Special Internet Connections List is a popular Web starting point because of the wide variety of Web sites and Internet services it offers. If you want to get a better idea of the wealth of information that's "out there," try making this list your home page for a while.

**http://info.cern.ch/hypertext/DataSources/Yanoff.html**

## SUSI Search Engine

SUSI is undoubtedly the best spider in the Web. SUSI stands for "Simple Unified Search Interface," and that's exactly what it is. Using fill-in-the-blank boxes, buttons and pull-down menus, SUSI lets you search about 40 of the Web's best information indexes. Chances are, if you can't find it here, you won't find it anywhere.
**http://web.nexor.co.uk/susi/susi.html**

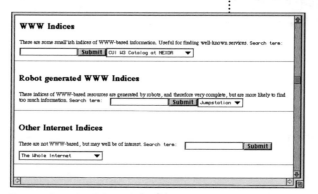

Figure 5-2: *SUSI's search engine.*

## The WebCrawler

The WebCrawler serves three functions: 1) it builds indexes for documents it finds on the Web, 2) it acts as a Net-wide agent, searching for documents of particular interest to the user and 3) it's a testbed for experimenting with Web search strategies.
**http://www.biotech.washington.edu/WebCrawler/ WebQuery.html**

The WebCrawler icon

## Wiretap Online Library

The Wiretap Online Library is an impressive collection of electronic texts. Everything's here—the classics, government reports and documents, humor, FAQ collections. Since the Online Library only exists as a Gopher site, you don't have the benefits of hypertext browsing and multimedia, but when you see what's available here, you'll probably be too overwhelmed to care.
**gopher://wiretap.spies.com/**

# Web Searching Tips

It's one thing to wander around the Web, discovering as you go, or running down a list of links that someone's given you. But what if you have something specific you're looking for, an obscure fact, a new trend, some demographic information? Here are some Web research tips that may help you:

- Know what you're looking for. Narrow down the search as closely as possible. Find out the appropriate terminology. Often, the most difficult part about finding something is figuring out what other people call it.

- Write down your best guesses of keywords and terminology before you get online. It's easy, especially in a hyperlinked environment, to get distracted. Stay on the trail of what you came for.

- Be organized! Keep track of were you've been so that you don't end up covering the same ground. Mosaic helps with this by changing the color of visited links, but it doesn't hurt to keep track of your searches. You can also keep a hotlink log of your session.

- Take notes as you go, using a notepad desk accessory or a resized (small) word processing window. You can cut and paste relevant material from the documents you're searching. Don't forget to match material you cut and paste with the document's URL in case you need to come back for more. Sometimes you get more useful information than you think you did. Going through your session notes, you may often find an excerpt you originally missed and you'll want to return to that document.

**HOT TIP**

Don't forget, you can use the Apple Scrapbook or Note Pad to cut and paste URLs you find while in Mosaic or while using other Internet services. That way, by saving them electronically and not writing them down, you remove the risk of copying them incorrectly.

- Don't put all your eggs in one basket. Often different Web search engines use different methods for organizing their indexes. Some are generated automatically, so they can include just about every Web page in existence. This is great, but you may spend a ridiculous amount of time sorting through a lot of useless information. On the other hand, some Web searching indexes are very specialized and won't ever have anything about the subject you're searching for. Diversify! Try to use a combination of techniques.
- Don't be lazy and just rely on webbed information. Sometimes it helps to use other Net resources. There's a lot of information out there on Gopher, WAIS, Archie and other searchable systems. If you're stuck in your Web searches, break out TurboGopher or Anarchie and start looking elsewhere.
- Don't be afraid to ask. Sometimes, other people are the best Internet search engines. Many people have been places you haven't; someone may have already surfed that elusive corner of the Net that has what you're looking for.
- USENET is also a great resource. Read newsgroups like comp.infosystems.www and other groups that have people with similar interests. A quick question on a newsgroup can reach thousands of people in minutes. Sometimes, you'll receive an answer within hours.

- Don't forget the phone book (and other more conventional methods). Often, the information you're looking for doesn't require a global data search as much as it does a call to your local library, TV station or government agency. The resources of the Net and the Web shouldn't end up being a crutch.

- Keep an open mind. Just because a source at first might not seem like it's going to be useful, learn to trust your instincts and break off the beaten path every once in a while—you might be surprised.

For additional words of wisdom gleaned from 23 professional data searchers, check out Reva Basch's *Secrets of the Super Searchers* (Eight Bit Books, 1993).

## Cool Sites to Visit

Now that we've seen what the Web has to offer in the way of resource centers and online libraries, it's time to expand our horizons and look at some of the more culturally oriented offerings. From art and pop culture to games and virtual reality, the sites in this section give you a bird's eye view of some of the Web's cooler watering holes.

### Art & Literature

One of the most exciting areas of the World Wide Web and hypermedia browsers like Mosaic is the possibilities they offer for making, exchanging and viewing art and literature over the Internet. A whole new type of art, called telematic art, has emerged in cyberspace. In telematic art, the Net and the Web themselves, and the forms of interactive communication they allow, become part of the art. You can learn more about telematic art, online art happenings, interactive literature and other cutting-edge forms of creativity at these sites. More traditional forms of art are well represented here, too.

## ANIMA: Arts Network for Integrated Media Applications

Billed as "the creative cultural information source," ANIMA is divided into sections covering events, electronic art magazines, online art projects and the tools and technologies used in contemporary art. A "Guide to Online Galleries" reviews online art projects and spaces and provides hotlinks to them.
**http://wimsey.com/anima/ANIMAhome.html**

Arts Network for Integrated Media

Figure 5-3: *ANIMA's logo.*

## Art/Images

A huge database of graphics and movies covering art, astronomy, geography, meteorology, natural sciences and politics.
**gopher://cs4sun.cs.ttu.edu/11/Art%20and%20Images**

## Art Links on the World Wide Web

Art galleries on the Web are scattered far and wide, but once found, they reveal an amazing amount of new and innovative art, music, video, photography and 3D renderings. This page contains links to most of the major and minor galleries on the Web.
**http://amanda.physics.wisc.edu/outside.html**

## CMU English Server

Located at Carnegie Mellon University (one of the largest, most influential continents in the online world), the English Server is a valuable resource to anyone interested in cultural theory and postmodernism. You'll find everything here from serious cultural criticism to the goofier sides of trendy academia (check out "Panic Bauldrillard"). There's enough here to keep you jacked in for days, so if you pay for your Net connection by the hour, make sure to set a timer before you dive in.
**http://english-server.hss.cmu.edu/**

## FineArt Forum

FineArt Forum is a monthly electronic newsletter covering art and technology. Besides the newsletter, they maintain a Gopher site, an online art gallery and a WWW resource directory.

**http://www.msstate.edu/Fineart_Online**

## *Jayhawk*

This is an archive for *Jayhawk*, a sci-fi novel by Mary K. Kuhner, originally posted to the Net in 144 installments. Here each part is available separately and each includes a story background.

**http://www.klab.caltech.edu/~flowers/jayhawk/**

## The OTIS Project

OTIS is a place for "image-makers and image-lovers to exchange ideas, collaborate and, in a loose sense of the word, meet." It is also a repository of images and information available for public perusal and participation. Exhibits of OTIS work have been held in cities around the globe.

**http://sunsite.unc.edu/otis/otis.html**

## Science Fiction Resource Guide

Probably the largest collection of science fiction literature in cyberspace. Contains articles, essays, interviews, bibliographies, FAQs, sci-fi journals and information on awards and conventions. Hotlinked to all the other major sci-fi Net nodes.

**ftp://gandalf.rutgers.edu/pub/sfl/sf-resource.guide.html**

Figure 5-4: *For anyone interested in cultural theory and postmodernism, visit CMU's English Server.*

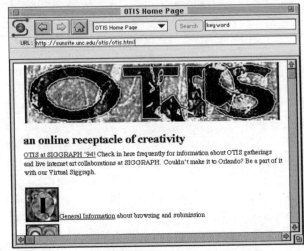

Figure 5-5: *The OTIS Home Page.*

## Search for Images in All of Gopherspace

Don't be fooled by the fact that when you access this Gopher site you get a blank screen labeled Searchable Gopher Index. Notice that the Search button has been activated. All you do is type in keywords and the Gopher searches for all images matching your request.
**gopher://info.mcc.ac.uk:2347/7-tgI%20-m2000%20**

## Worldwide Web Art Navigator

A collection of brief descriptions of hotlinked sites to "get you started on your quest for art in the labyrinth of the Web."
**http://www.uiah.fi/isea/navigator.html**

## Le WebLouvre

That's right, the world-famous French art museum is online. They are currently hosting three exhibits: a French medieval art demonstration, a collection of well-known paintings from famous artists and a tour around Paris, the Eiffel Tower and the Champs-Elysees.
**http://mistral.enst.fr/~pioch/louvre/**

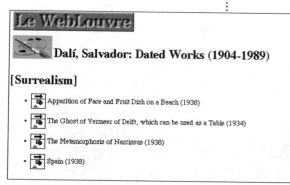

Figure 5-6: *Salvador Dali on Le WebLouvre.*

## Commerce

All eyes in cyberspace are turned toward the emerging world of Net-based commerce. Some people are excited by the prospect of doing business over the Internet, others loathe the idea, thinking it will turn it into a virtual strip mall. The bottom line is that commerce in this realm is inevitable and platforms like Mosaic are ideally suited for the online marketplace. The sites in this section represent some of the first store-fronts to hang out their "Open For Business" signs.

## EINet Galaxy Homepage

This is the home page for EINet, an Internet service provider. Light on the promotional material, it is also a vital link to a number of Net resources organized by subject. You can even download MacWeb, EINet's answer to Mosaic.
**http://galaxy.einet.net/galaxy.html**

## The Internet Mall

A budding commercial Net enterprise with several dozen "stores" selling media items, personal items, computer wares, books and various services.
**http://www.kei.com/internet-mall.html**

## Internet Shopping Network

Now you can "shop till you drop" at the virtual mall! On the leading edge of Net commercialization, the Internet Shopping Network offers a way to electronically shop for just about anything your heart desires. To get started, send them your credit card number and they send you an ISN password. After that, you find what you want, grab the virtual goods and the real-world equivalents are delivered to your door. I couldn't find the commemorative Star Trek: The Next Generation Borg plates, but I'm *sure* they're here somewhere.
**http://shop.internet.net/**

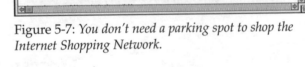

Figure 5-7: *You don't need a parking spot to shop the Internet Shopping Network.*

## MarketPlace.com

Another burgeoning commercial site on the Internet. MarketPlace.com wants to offer the Internet community a convenient and useful online shopping environment. So far they have about eight "storefronts" occupied.
**http://marketplace.com**

## Computer Resources

If you want to stay abreast of news and information related to your computer, take a peek at these excellent resources.

### Robert Lentz's Macintosh Resources

Bob Lentz has obviously spent a lot of time combing the globe for Mac-related resources so you don't have to. Here you'll find lists of Mac FTP sites, publication archives, product information and just about everything else that exists on the Web for the benefit of Mac owners.
http://www.astro.nwu.edu/lentz/mac/home-mac.html

### What's New on comp.infosystems.announce?

The kind folks at Rochester have automated the process of keeping up on all the new Web pages as they're announced. Rather than having to spend several hours a day scanning and archiving all the new site announcements on comp.infosystems.announce, What's New scans USENET automatically and lists each new resource as soon as it hits the Net. Each listing is hyperlinked to the page announced for quick and easy Net surfing.
http://www.cs.rochester.edu/users/grads/ferguson/announce/

### Ventana Visitors Center

Check out the latest news and information about Mosaic and get updates on this book. The Visitors Center contains hypertext WWW information and also supports *The Mac Internet Tour Guide* and the *Internet Membership Kit*. A great source of MacTCP-related freeware and shareware.
http://www.vmedia.com/vvc

## Cyberculture

Cyberculture is what you get when you cross digital technologies, avant-pop culture and fringe science. Inspired by the cyberpunk science fiction of writers like William Gibson and Bruce Sterling, cyberculture is concerned with the near future and how the increasing and widespread availability of high technology will affect our lives. It's a do-it-yourself mentality applied to futurism.

## CyberNet

The Webmasters at CyberNet believe that the Internet has gotten far too boring, that it's lost its pioneering edge. They are dedicated to preserving "the unconventional nature of the Internet." They include a lengthy list of Web sites pushing the edges of art, science, culture and taste.
**http://venus.mcs.com/~flowers/html/gcybernet.html**

## Cyberpoet's Guide to Virtual Culture

Those who are interested in learning more about "cyberculture," the nexus of pop culture, high technology and fringe science, should check out Cyberpoet's Guide to Virtual Culture. This is a popular watering hole for cybernauts. Includes essays on various aspects of cyberculture, a cyberspace lexicon and dictionary, and a huge hotlinked database of art, pop culture, cyberculture, music, electronic magazines and more.
**http://128.230.38.86/cgvc/cgvc1.htm**

 **Funky**. Shake your booty!

 **Hazardous**. May cause brain damage.

 **Kitsch**. Oh, how very lovely.

 **Noise**. Boom, boom, boom, twang!

 **Populaire Culture**. Putting the pop back in culture.

Figure 5-8: *CyberNet's HotLink icons.*

## Electronic Cafe

The Electronic Cafe (or "ecafe" to its regulars) is a place to explore music, art, literature and virtual community. It's a place for people to meet, learn, share ideas and come together in ways that only the Net can make possible.
**http://www.cyberspace.org/u/ecafe/www/index.html**

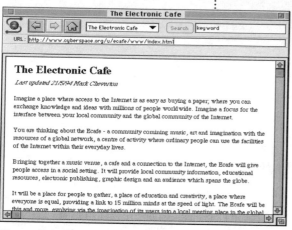

Figure 5-9: *You can get anything you want at the Electronic Cafe.*

## FringeWare

FringeWare is a company and Net-based community dedicated to creating an alternative marketplace for goods and services offered by Net citizens. They publish a catalog of hard-to-find software, hardware and cybercultural curios, and two magazines: *FringeWare Review* and *Unshaved Truths*. They also maintain an Internet-wide mailing list and discussion groups on cyberculture and alternative economics.
**http://io.com/commercial/fringeware/home.html**

## NCSA Virtual Reality Lab

The NCSA Virtual Reality Laboratory is a research facility exploring new methods of visualizing and interfacing with scientific data and simulations. The lab is located in the Beckman Institute for Advanced Science and Technology on the University of Illinois campus. The goal of the lab is to study and use improved methods of viewing and interacting with information. The VR Lab's Web site contains papers related to their research and project reports, with graphics and links to FTP sites, and USENET newsgroups devoted to virtual reality and other advanced imaging technologies.
**http://www.ncsa.uiuc.edu/VR/VR/VRHomePage.html**

When logging onto FTP sites, it's a good idea to keep in mind
what time zone you're calling. Logging into a university computer
during peak school hours may leave you waiting in a long virtual
line, twiddling your thumbs. Try another site where it's the
middle of the night and you may have better luck. Popular information services usually have less traffic during the day and are
more crowded right after school and work and on weekends.
Also, whenever possible, try the sites closest to you first. Calling
France or Sweden when you can get what you need from  a local
Internet site is wasting somebody's money, possibly your tax
dollars. Be a considerate Net citizen.

## neXus Home Page

neXus contains information and links that lean heavily toward the
more "cyberpunk" edges of the Net. You'll find links to rave culture
and music, hacking and the computer underground, industrial music
and the well-known electronic compendium of cyberculture, the
FutureCulture FAQ.
**http://www.cis.ksu.edu/~solder/nexus.html**

## UK VR-SIG

This site provides access to the UK Virtual Reality Special Interest
Group (UK VR-SIG) and is a major link point to VR archives and
discussion groups throughout the Internet. If you're interested in
virtual reality, this is the place to go to connect with the VR community
online. Get information on upcoming events, new research and development, and the latest software; view demos; and much more.
**http://pipkin.lut.ac.uk/WWWdocs/LUTCHI/people/sean/vr-sig/vr-si.html**

## Electronic Newsstands

As mentioned in Chapter 1, a significant part of Mosaic's future will likely be in online publishing. The software and communications hardware are not yet up to par, but the neccessary innovations are just around the corner. To get a peek at the first wave of magazines that have set up newsstands in cyberspace, check out some of the following.

### bOING bOING

*bOING bOING* has brazenly dubbed itself "The World's Greatest Neurozine." In its quarterly print form it covers the wild and wacky fringes of pop and cyberculture. The new bOING bOING Online features an art gallery (mainly of comic art), articles from past issues and online exclusives. Excerpts from *bOING bOING*'s first book *The Happy Mutant Handbook* (Putnam/Berkeley, 1995) will soon be appearing online.
**http://www.zeitgeist.net/public/Boing-boing/bbw3/boing.boing.html**

### *Fishnet* Homepage

This home page is the site for an amazing one-man Internet sideshow. *Fishnet* is a weekly publication that gleans some of the best and most interesting items from the Net and stirs them together into a spicy infostew. Here you can browse back issues by date or see a list of all the subjects that *Fishnet* has covered.
**http://www.cs.washington.edu/homes/pauld/fishnet**

Figure 5-10: *Stroll through* bOING bOING's *art gallery.*

## Global Network Navigator

GNN is a series of publications and information services provided by O'Reilly & Associates, the computer book publishers. From the GNN Home Page you can access *GNN NetNews*, a weekly publication of news from the Internet, *GNN Magazine*, a quarterly with feature articles, how-to's, reviews of Net resources and an advice and commentary section, the electronic version of the *Whole Internet Catalog*, with hotlinks to all of its resource listings, an "arcade," a travel center and The Internet Center, which includes a Help Desk for new Net citizens. You have to subscribe to GNN, but the subscription is free of charge.

Figure 5-11: *GNN's Home Page.*

http://nearnet.gnn.com/gnn/gnn.html

## Hypermedia Zine List

Zines (small, do-it-yourself publications on any topic of interest) have moved onto the Net. But, like their tiny-circulation print cousins, electronic zines (or e-zines) can be incredibly hard to find. Luckily, there's a one-stop shop for electronic zine access, the Hypermedia Zine List. The list also includes links to USENET newsgroups about zines, other zine archives and even a list of zines that are readable on the Web.

http://www.acns.nwu.edu/ezines/

## Medialist

A database of email addresses for major daily newspapers, magazines, TV and radio stations, etc. Many of the entries for the newspapers and magazines include email addresses for the section and column editors (Op Ed page, Letters, Arts, Story Ideas, etc.).

ftp://ftp.std.com/customers/periodicals/Middlesex-News/medialist

## Mother Jones

The Web site for *Mother Jones*, the radical expose magazine, has back issues and material related to the magazine and its mission.
**http://www.mojones.com/motherjones.html**

## *PCWeek* Best News Sources & Online Mags

The *PCWeek* page is a news junkie's paradise. Nowhere else on the Net can you browse the *San Francisco Examiner* and *Chronicle*, USENET FAQs, the NASDAQ Financial Executive, *PowerPC News* and others, all from the same site. Don't be fooled though—even *PCWeek* wants to have some fun every once in a while! You can link to Adam Curry's The Vibe music server, *InterText* online fiction and other recreational sites.
**ftp://www.ziff.com/~pcweek/best_news.html**

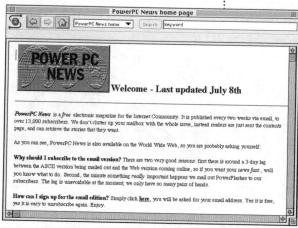

Figure 5-12: PowerPC News *home page.*

## PowerPC News

The latest news on the PowerPC, along with some of the most up-to-date and interesting information about the Internet and personal computing and technology in general. You can get it mailed directly to your email account, or you can wait a couple of days and read it here as a Web text.
**http://power.globalnews.com/**

## TidBITS

Adam C. Engst's *TidBITS* is one of the best documents to whiz through cyberspace. Published weekly, it covers a broad wavefront of computer hardware, software and industry news and reviews (mostly from a Mac perspective). The Web site features an index of back issues and the current issue in HTML form. One neat feature is that references within an issue to past articles in *TidBITS* are hotlinked.

**http://www.dartmouth.edu/Pages/TidBITS/TidBITS.html**

## *USA Today* Headline News, Sports, etc...

You can telnet from Mosaic (if you have NCSA Telnet installed) and read the day's issue of *USA Today*. You have to obtain an account before you're able to access the paper, but the account is free.

**telnet freenet-in-a.cwru.edu**
**telnet freenet-in-b.cwru.edu**
**telnet freenet-in-c.cwru.edu**
**Login as: visitor**

## Webster's Weekly

*Webster's Weekly* is a weekly features magazine published exclusively on the Web. It has columns on music and movies; politics and psychology; mad rantings and humor. Published every Wednesday.

**http://www.awa.com/w2/**

Figure 5-13: *A sneak peek at* Webster's Weekly.

## Wired

*Wired* is one of the most exciting new magazines to appear in years. It combines a progressive, youthful design with hard-hitting journalism from the cutting edge of digital culture and technology. Since its beginning, *Wired* has been interested in maintaining a vital presence in cyberspace. Although that involvement has so far been limited to the tools that are already available (with forums on AOL, The WELL and USENET), *Wired* is currently working on pushing the envelope of Net-based publishing. They have big plans for a new @Wired service that is currently under construction. Find out about their upcoming plans and read *Wired* back issues and special Net "Extras" at the *Wired* WWW site. **http://www.wired.com**

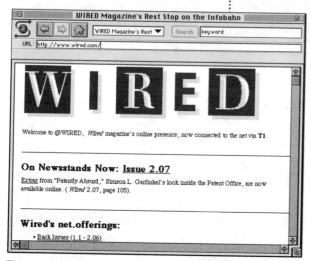

Figure 5-14: Wired *Magazine's Rest Stop on the Infobahn.*

## 3W

*3W* is a bi-monthly British magazine devoted to the Internet and the World Wide Web. Their Web site contains excerpts from the print magazine and information about past and upcoming issues. **http://www.3W.com/3W/**

## Fun & Games

Whether it's sports, board or role-playing games, or comedy that you're looking for, the Web has something to offer. The Net has even spawned its own brand of humor as exemplified by the Internet coffee machine and, would you believe, an Internet hottub?

### Advanced Dungeons & Dragons & Other Role-Playing Games (RPGs)

Links to game-related newsgroups, FTP sites, MUDs (role-playing games played on the Net) and other gaming Web sites. Also includes a small fantasy art gallery.
**http://www.acm.uiuc.edu/duff/index.html**

### BU's Interactive WWW Games

The first interactive multiplayer games page on the Web. Play against a computer in a game of tic-tac-toe or pegs, try to solve the 9-puzzle—the sliding tiles game—or risk your virtual life playing Hunt The Wumpus in real time against other denizens of the Net. Things are a bit primitive at this point, but it's a harbinger of things to come.
**http://www.bu.edu/Games/games.html**

### Doctor Fun

Doctor Fun is a single-panel cartoon by David Farley distributed every weekday over the Internet. Doctor Fun has been in production since September 1993. The cartoons are rendered in vivid colors and uploaded to the Net as 24-bit JPEG images. Farley's work has appeared in *Spy*, *Punch* and *Campus Life*, and he has done work for King Features and Recycled Paper Products.
**http://sunsite.unc.edu/Dave/drfun.html**

Figure 5-15: *Make your day with a cartoon from Doctor Fun.*

## Games Domain

Contains links to game FAQs, FTP sites, Web pages and other Net resources related to game playing.
**http://wcl-rs.bham.ac.uk/~djh/index.html**

## Internet Coffee Machine

It's late in the day, you've been Web walking for hours and boy are your hands tired. You want a little pick-me-up, but you don't want the nagging jitters of caffeine. How about a virtual cup o' joe? One at a safe distance—say—the United Kingdom? The Trojan Room Coffee Pot lives at the University of Cambridge in England. A special camera is trained on the pot, taking a picture of it every second. That picture is then digitized and made available to the Cambridge Web server. By typing the URL below, you can access the currently available image to see how much coffee is in the pot. This is a sophisticated upgrade on another nerdly Net gag called the Internet Coke Machine. A number of university computer sciences departments have wired their soda machines so that anyone on the Net can query them to find out how many sodas are currently available. To access the Coke machines you need to use the Finger command. If you know how to do this (see the "Finger" section in Chapter 4), try fingering drink@drink.csh.rit.edu.
**http://www.cl.cam.ac.uk/coffee/coffee.html**

**Aliens Have Invaded Cyberspace!** Bill Barker was a gallery artist living in Reno, Nevada, when in 1992, someone gave him a reprint of a bizarre article on alien invasion and abduction. He became fascinated with the subject and people's seemingly sincere tales of flying saucers and aliens among us. With tongue firmly planted in cheek, Barker began doing a series of stark black-and-white drawings, using an alien motif. He saw this as an interesting way to speak about "alienation" in all of its forms and the fears that people have about being controlled by unseen forces. The response to Barker's work, done behind the mask of a mysterious entity called the Schwa Corporation, has been phenomenal. Barker has developed a line of "alien defense products" based on his Schwa characters and themes, and these items are hot. He's developing a whole line of cheap alien objets d'art and has even been approached by a toy and a clothing company who are tickled by his strange sense of humor and his almond-headed aliens with the big not-so-friendly eyes.

The Schwa Corporation now has a headquarters on the World Wide Web. Point your URL at: http://www.scs.unr.edu/homepage/rory/schwa/schwa.html

## Internet Hot Tub

If you think the Internet coffee and Coke machines are silly, how about the Internet Hot Tub! That's right, someone in Ann Arbor, Michigan, has their outdoor hot tub connected to a Sun Workstation. By sending email to the tub, you can find out how it's doing.
**email: hottub@hamjudo.mi.org**

## The Nando X Baseball Server

The Nando X Baseball Server contains baseball news, commentary, box scores, history, graphics and even videos.
**http://www.nando.net/baseball/bbserv.html**

## Snapshots From the UMBC Computer Department

Probably in any other context, pictures like this would bore you to death. However, having the ability to snoop in on someone's office hundreds or even thousands of miles away *does* have its appeal. Here are up-to-the-minute snapshots of what's going on in the computer department at the University of Maryland, Baltimore. The pictures are relatively small and in GIF format, so even if you have a low-powered Mac and a SLIP connection, you can still snoop. Take a peek.
**http://www.cs.umbc.edu/video_snapshots/**

## USENET Rec.Humor Page

This page contains excerpts from the rec.humor USENET newsgroups, it also contains top ten lists, tasteless jokes, song spoofs, goofy headlines and links to other humor-related sites.
**http://www.cs.odu.edu/~cashman/humor.html**

**Internet Hot Tub Update**
Date: 94-04-01 13:22:53 est
Subj: Hottub status from hottub@hamjudo .mi.org

Paul's hottub is nice and warm at about 101 degrees Fahrenheit. It is cold outside at about 51 degrees Fahrenheit. The ozone generator is working. The cover is closed. The access door is open. The backup battery is OK at 10.6 volts (this will still work down to 6 volts).

**Welcome to the Baseball Server**

Figure 5-16: *Welcome to the Nando X Baseball Server.*

## Kids

Kids are obviously having fun with Mosaic and WWW, too. Hypertext Markup Language is easy enough that, with help from an adult, kids can create their own Web pages and attach sound and image files to them. Here are a few samples of kids showing their talents online. The Kids On Campus Internet Tour is a great way to introduce kids to the Net.

Figure 5-17: *Some signs found on the Kids On Campus site.*

### SchoolHouse Gopher Server

Not pretty by WWW standards, but this Gopher site is a great resource for kids and teachers. A lot of links here.
**http://crusher.bev.net:70/1/Schoolhouse/kids**

### Spanish Counting Books

Mr. Buckman and his students created a very cute book to teach kids how to count in Spanish. The pages were drawn by his kindergarten students using KidPics. There are audio links that let you hear the students reading the numbers out loud. You can even download an entire self-running slide show of the project.
**http://davinci.vancouver.wsu.edu/buckman/ SpanishBook.html**

### Kids On Campus Internet Tour

Every year, the Cornell Theory Center has a Kids On Campus day where kids and computers come together. The theme for the 1994 day was "Navigating the Information Superhighway," and the folks at Cornell created this huge image map of street signs to guide the kids through the various Net resources available to them. Plunk the little ones down in front of this and let 'em go to town!
**http://www.tc.cornell.edu:80/Kids.on.Campus/KOC94**

## Miscellaneous

Here's a category for things that refused to fit into any of the other categories. Gotcha!

## Best of the Net

*GNN Magazine*'s annual awards for the overall best Web pages. Looking at these "best of" lists is very helpful when designing your own pages for Web-wide consumption.
**http://src.doc.ic.ac.uk/gnn/meta/internet/ feat/best.html**

## Best of the Web

The Best of the Web Awards is an annual contest that gives awards to Web pages that exhibit "the quality, versatility, and power of the World Wide Web." They see their mission as two-fold:

- Promote the Web to new/potential users by showing its highlights.
- Help information providers see what they can do with HTML/HTTP.

The '94 awards were selected via a two-month open nomination period, and a two-week open voting period. The awards were first announced at the International W3 Conference in Geneva on May 26, 1994. The awards are now on permanent display at the URL listed above. Hotlinks are provided to the 14 award winners and all the runners up, making this single site a major access point to dozens of the best sites and sounds in cyberspace.
**http://wings.buffalo.edu/contest/**

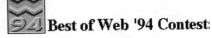

**Best of Web '94 Contest**:
The Best of the Web logo

## Canadian Radio

An experimental database containing sound and text files from The Canadian Broadcasting Corporation. Popular programs such as Quirks and Quarks, Basic Black and Sunday Morning can be heard online. Obviously these sound files are huge and you probably need to have a direct Internet connection to make downloading them cost effective. Ordering information is available to buy the programs on cassette tape. **http://debra.dgbt.doc.ca/cbc/cbc.html**

## Cool Stuff in the Internet

Here's where you'll find some of the hippest links to video and multimedia on the Web. If you have a hardwired Net connection and are running X Windows on your Mac, or if you have access to an X Windows system, check out the Video Browser at MIT for a glimpse of video on demand. **http://www.cs.ucdavis.edu/internet_stuff.html**

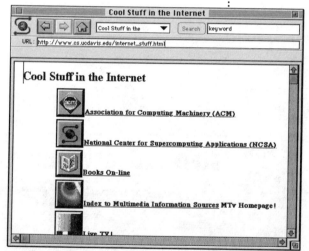

Figure 5-18: *Some of the hippest places to visit are found on the Cool Stuff in the Internet site.*

## Music, Film & Television

Music and moving pictures have so far not made it big in cyberspace. Powerful direct-connected machines do OK with audio and video, but for SLIP/PPP connections, at today's modem speeds, music and film can only be hinted at. The sites in this section are either pathbreaking attempts at showing what the Web can do in this area, or they're repositories of information on more traditional forms of music, film and television.

## Cardiff's Movie Database Browser

A huge database of movie information, presented in an easy-to-search format. You can look up films by title, actor or even by quotes. Can't figure out what to rent at the video store tonight? Stop in here first and have a look around. Remember a famous line but can't put your finger on who said it and in what film? Search by the quotation. A film buff's dream come true.
http://www.cm.cf.ac.uk/Movies/

## Internet Underground Music Archive

IUMA sports great graphics and award-winning page design (Best of the Net '94) and provides an innovative service to the Net music community. The Archive gives needed exposure to little-known bands, providing bios, commentary and reviews, and audio excerpts. Legal issues around music and music on the Internet are also covered. The musical excerpts are available in MPEG format only, which is unfortunate since there are currently no MPEG audio players available for the Mac. There are two such applications in the works: Audition Lite by Aware Corp. and a piece of shareware being developed by G. T. Warner of AT&T. One or both of these may be available by the time you read this.
http://sunsite.unc.edu/ianc/index.html

Figure 5-19: *The Internet Underground Music Archive.*

## Kaleidospace

Kaleidospace is devoted to the promotion, distribution and placement of independent artists, musicians, performers, CD-ROM authors, writers, animators and filmmakers. Artists provide samples of their work, which Kaleidospace integrates into a multimedia document. Artists pay flat rentals to showcase their work; Internet users may order from the artists online, as well as by phone, fax, email and snail mail. Kaleidospace provides placement for artists wishing to showcase

their work to agents, directors, gallery owners, publishers, record labels and other industry professionals. Kaleidospace also offers Gopher and FTP services at Gopher.kspace.com and ftp.kspace.com, respectively. **http://kspace.com/**

Figure 5-20: *A picture from the popular TV show "Mystery Science Theater 3000."*

## Deus Ex Machina: Mystery Science Theater 3000

Deux Ex Machina is a meta-home page linking all of the Web-accessible documents about the popular TV show "Mystery Science Theater 3000." Animations, MST3K newsletters, pictures, sounds, show schedules, etc., are all available through this "gateway." You'll be astonished by how many sites around the Internet have MST3K-related material.

**http://128.194.15.32/~dml601a/mst3k/mst3k.html**

## Adam Curry's The Vibe

Former MTV VJ Adam Curry has had his share of problems in cyberspace. He is currently being sued by MTV for using the Internet site name mtv.com. He's now changed his address to the one below where he maintains a number of services, one called The Vibe, which has music reviews, commentary, musician interviews, concert information, chart action and back issues of Curry's electronic gossip sheet *The*

*Cyber-Sleaze Report.* Adam Curry's Recording Studio offers musical selections that can be downloaded. There are also links to Web pages devoted to different rock artists.
**http://metaverse.com/vibe/index.html**

Adam Curry's The Vibe logo

## Pop Culture

Today's pop culture is drenched in technology, so it's not surprising to find cutting-edge expressions of youth culture on the Web. If you're looking to find out what today's youth are thinking and feeling, and what they're doing to express themselves, check out these two sites. The Web's Edge will connect you to many other interesting places.

## Alternative X

Alternative X is an electronic publishing company focused on the '90s alternative/countercultural scene. Founded by "avant-pop" novelist, musician and essayist Mark Amerika, Alternative X's purpose is to "feature publications created by people who are actively engaged in the world of alternative art, writing, music, philosophy, electronic media and anything/everything else that might interest the emerging generation of creative thinkers and doers."
**http://marketplace.com/0/alt.x/althome.html**

## Underworld Industries' "Web's Edge"

Underworld Industries' "Cultural Playground" is the home of Under-world Industries—a group dedicated to linking underground music, art and the Internet.
**http://kzsu.stanford.edu/uwi.html**

## Telecommunications Policy & Information Law

Telecommunications and information law are exciting legal arenas these days. There are major commercial forces amassing on the edges of cyberspace (the cable/interactive TV industries, the phone companies, the multimedia vendors) and border skirmishes are already breaking out. While on another front, all the old rules about intellectual property, information theft and copyrights are being called into question in our digital age. If you want to watch the fur fly, or if you want to get involved in trying to steer the course of these emerging policies and laws, the sites in this section are key points of access.

### Information Law Alert

Information Law Alert is the authoritative online source for news on legal disputes involving intellectual property, wireless communications and telecommunications.
gopher://marketplace.com/11/ila

### Electronic Frontier Foundation

The Electronic Frontier Foundation (EFF) was founded in July 1990 to ensure that the principles embodied in the U.S. Constitution and the Bill of Rights are protected as new communications technologies emerge. EFF has been at work since then, through education, legal council and public debate, helping to shape the nation's communications policies and infrastructure. Their ultimate goal is nothing less than the creation of an electronic democracy. The EFF Gopher site contains many of their papers, articles, newsletters, action alerts and organizational materials. Other publications related to computer culture and legal issues are also stored here, as is the EFF's *Guide to the Internet*.
gopher://gopher.eff.org/00/about.eff

## FCC Gopher

This is the FCC's archive of articles, releases and documents related to communications.
**gopher://gopher.fcc.gov/**

## The Legal Domain Network

This Web site is a repository for legal information on the Internet. Here you can gain access to all the law-related USENET discussion groups such as law, alt.dear.whitehouse, alt.freedom.of.information.act, alt.politics, comp.org.eff (the Electronic Frontier Foundation), misc.int-property (intellectual property rights) and misc.legal.
**http://www.kentlaw.edu/lawnet/lawnet.html**

## Pepper and Corazzini, L.L.P

Pepper and Corazzini, L.L.P., is a law firm specializing in communications law. Its practice covers radio, television, cable, satellite, MMDS, radio common carrier and cellular matters. Their law offices online include a very useful series of articles on issues surrounding telecom and information law.
**http://www.iis.com/p-and-c**

## Travel

Before embarking on a trip, it's always wise to look through your maps and travel guides. You were smart enough to realize this when you bought *Mosaic Quick Tour* before trekking off into the wilderlands of the Web. The next time you manage to peel yourself away from the computer to take a real world journey, why not consult the following resources for the travel information you'll need. Be a smart traveler—don't go to Singapore with graffiti on your mind.

### The Rec.Travel Library

A library of information for travelers maintained at the University of Manitoba, in Winnipeg, Manitoba, Canada. Approximately 15mb of travel information. Most of the information is sorted by continent and country, plus general travel info, cruise reviews, addresses and phone numbers for tourism offices worldwide, and pointers to other Internet resources.
**ftp://ftp.cc.umanitoba.ca/rec-travel**

### Travel Information

A one-stop shop to some of the travel information found on the Net. Airline info, FAQs about tourism, specific information on countries and cities around the world, travel guides and newsletters.
**http://galaxy.einet.net/GJ/travel.html**

## Moving On

As I write this, today's *Washington Post* has an article on the bright and profitable future of Mosaic. The piece claims that while Mosaic is a "path-breaking navigation program," it is difficult to use and so "prone to glitches" that a number of companies are having to step in and refine the program for widespread use. While it may be the case that commercial versions of Mosaic will make wonderful additions and improvements, suggesting that it needs serious work before the masses can use it is misleading. Mosaic's current popularity is due directly to the fact that it *isn't* hard to use, and certainly it's as reliable as a number of the information services I subscribe to. Hopefully, as Mosaic and the commerce around it grows, the free version will not be left behind. There's always something more exciting about using software this powerful that you didn't have to pay for (and you didn't pirate).

So there you have it my friends, Mosaic and the World Wide Web in a few easy lessons and some enjoyable datastrolls. Hopefully you now have enough knowledge and experience to be a confident and resourceful Web user. If you're still feeling unsure of yourself, or just want to expand your knowledge on the Net and the Web, I suggest you travel to some of the Web sites listed in the "General Net Resources" section above. Between those resources and the various indexes and robots available in the "Robot Librarian" section, you should have no trouble finding what you need in cyberspace. Mosaic brings an unprecedented level of access to the information and ideas found on the Net. As you become more comfortable with it, the program will move into the background and all that it offers will move forward.

# APPENDIX
## MOSAIC 2.X'S IMPROVEMENTS

As this book is being written, the Internet community is excited over the public release of the much-anticipated Mosaic 2.x. Alpha versions of 2.x are quickly making their way across the Net. A full-blown 2.0 release will hopefully be available by the time you read this book. Here is a rundown of some of the new and improved features you'll find in Mosaic 2.x.

### Forms

The addition of "fill-in-the-blank" boxes and forms allows Web documents to include data input fields and other ways of making documents interactive. As more commercial entities begin using Mosaic, this will be an increasingly valuable feature. One criticism people have had of the Mac version of Mosaic has been its lack of interactive capabilities. Now users will be able to post comments, fill-in surveys and enter credit information through the forms feature.

### Tables

Mosaic 2.x has added the ability to display table-based information and charts inside Web documents.

## Type Style Additions

Strikethrough, Superscript and Subscript styles have been added.

## Improved Error Reporting

Fancier, more informative dialog boxes will help communicate errors.

## Improved Pagination

Improvements in pagination speed, layout, added white space and numerous other fixes.

## User-Configurable Background Color

The User-Configurable Background Color will allow you to change the background color of the Mosaic document window.

## New Hotlist Interface

A full-featured pop-up window of Hotlist controls has been added.

## Custom Menus

The new Custom Menus give you the ability to create custom pull-down menus.

## Quick Keys

More command key sequences have been added.

## Firewall Proxy Support

Firewall support, including CERN Proxy and SOCKS services.

## URL Entries

It has long been a mystery as to why users can't type URLs into the URL box and be able to activate links from there (rather than having to invoke the Open URL... command). Now you can!

## Open URL

Mosaic now remembers the last URL entered in the Open URL window. In Mosaic 1.x, if you close the URL box, the last-typed URL is lost. In 2.x, since the previous address is remembered, now, at least, you don't have to retype http:// each time.

## Use This URL for Home

New Options menu item. Allows you to select the current document to be used as the new home page. This new page is automatically recorded in your Preferences file.

## ODOC Event Support & AppleScript Open URL Support

ODOC is the Open Document standard that Apple will be releasing in the fall. Open URL support will allow another application to tell Mosaic what URL to open.

## Use Header Mode

This feature allows you to get additional information about a link without having to connect to it. The information, which includes file type, modification date, file size and server information appears in a pop-up window.

## Preferences Window

This window was completely redesigned to make modifications easier. Four subwindows can now be selected: Misc, Links, Dirs and Gates.

## Global History List

Mosaic now maintains a history of links between sessions. You can determine the number of entries that can be included in this list, or choose to remove files from the list that are older than a certain number of days. This is not related to the session history list.

## Speech Recognition

With Apple's Speech Recognition Extension installed, Mosaic 2.x will respond to a series of voice commands.

## Mosaic 2.x's Changes

The most striking changes in 2.x are cosmetic, with more of a "polished," heavy-on-the-grayscales look. Also, the program seems to be moving toward greater organization, flexibility and ease of use. Most of the changes to the inner workings of Mac Mosaic 2.x are bringing it more in line with X Windows Mosaic, i.e., Forms and Tables support, an additional History feature and script capabilities. The addition of Forms for Mac Mosaic is much needed, as more Web sites are creating increasingly interactive documents.

The size/memory differences between Mosaic 1 and 2 can be seen in the table below.

| Version | Actual Size | Memory Requirements |
|---------|-------------|---------------------|
| Mac Mosaic 1.0.3 | 828k | 2mb of RAM recommended |
| Mac Mosaic 2.0A | 1.3mb | 3mb of RAM recommended |

Table A-1: *Size/Memory Differences between Mosaic 1 and 2.*

# QUICK-REFERENCE PAGE

## Keyboard Command Chart

| Menu | Item | Keyboard Combination |
|---|---|---|
| File | New Window | Command+N |
| | Open URL | Command+U |
| | Close | Command+W |
| | Print | Command+P |
| | Mail Developers | Command+M |
| | Quit | Command+Q |
| Edit | Undo | Command+Z |
| | Cut | Command+X |
| | Copy | Command+C |
| | Paste | Command+V |
| | Find | Command+F |
| | Find Again | Command+G |
| Options | Load to Disk | Command+L |
| | Auto-Load Images | Command+I |
| | Preferences | Command+; |
| | Styles | Command+T |
| Navigate | Back | Command+[ |
| | Forward | Command+] |
| | Home | Command+H |
| | Hotlist | Command+J |
| | Add this Document | Command+D |

## Useful Email Addresses

Mac Mosaic Tech Support          mmosaic@ncsa.uiuc.edu

_____          _____

_____          _____

## Nifty Web Sites

Ventana Online                   http://www.vmedia.com

_____          _____

_____          _____

## Useful FTP Sites

Ventana Online                   ftp://ftp.vmedia.com
NCSA                             ftp://ftp.ncsa.uiuc.edu
University of North Carolina     ftp://sunsite.unc.edu
Stanford University              ftp://sumex-aim.stanford.edu
University of Michigan           ftp://mac.archive.umich.edu

## Technical Help

Built into Mosaic is a Mail Developers feature. If you've put your return email address in the Preferences box, then by choosing Mail Developers (or Command+M), you can send technical questions or suggestions to the makers of Mosaic.

You can also write:
Software Development Group
NCSA Mosaic for Macintosh
152 Computing Applications Bldg.
605 East Springfield Avenue
Champaign, IL 61820-5518

# GLOSSARY

**Anchors**   In version 1.x of Mosaic, hyperlinks were referred to as *anchors*. In version 2.x they are called *hotlinks*. Also anchor colors have become hotlink colors.

**Annotations**   Personal messages, in either text or audio form, that can be attached to your Web documents in Mosaic. The notes do not effect the actual document, but are available to you whenever that document is viewed.

**Archie**   A Net-based service that allows one to locate files that are available for downloading via FTP.

**AU sounds**   A type of audio format used in Mosaic.

**BinHex**   A file conversion format that converts binary files to ASCII text files.

**Client**   A computer that has access to services over a computer network. The computer that can be accessed by a client is called a *server*. Once connected, the client can access the various services the server offers (e.g., FTP, Gopher, etc.).

**Client/server architecture**   The client/server scheme works by having a client program (Mosaic) connect to a server program on a host computer. The client program sends requests to the server, which then takes the information request, disconnects from the client, processes the request and then reconnects to the client program to send the requested info back. This is in contrast with traditional Internet databases where you connect to them remotely (via telnet or some other form of connection), and then proceed to actually run the program from the remote site.

**Cyberspace**   Word coined by sci-fi writer William Gibson to refer to a near-future computer network where users can mentally travel through matrices of data. The term is now often used to describe today's Internet.

**Dial-up connection**   A connection from your computer to a host Internet-connected computer over standard phone lines. Dial up is currently the most popular form of Net connection for the home user.

**Direct connection**   A permanent connection between your computer system (either a single CPU or a LAN) and the Internet. This is also called a *leased line connection* because you are leasing the telephone connection from the phone company. A direct connection is in contrast to a SLIP/PPP or dial-up connections.

**Document**   In the World Wide Web, a document refers to any file, whether containing text, media or hyperlinks, that can be transferred from an HTTP server to a client program (such as Mosaic).

**Document window**   In Mosaic, the scrollable window where HTML documents can be viewed is commonly referred to as the *document window.*

**Eudora**   A freeware email program that can be used over a MacTCP connection. Eudora is a great piece of freeware that was originally developed by Steve Dorner at the University of Illinois.

**External viewer**   Program used for presenting graphics, audio and movies in Mosaic. The word viewer is a bit confusing since external viewer also refers to audio applications. Helper applications, the other term used for these external programs, seems more appropriate.

**E-zines**   Electronic zines, or small circulation publications, that are distributed over computer networks. The word "zines" comes from the print world where it is used to describe small, do-it-yourself publications.

**FAQ (Frequently Asked Questions)**   A text file on the Internet that answers commonly asked questions on a given subject. FAQs are a major source of Net knowledge and wisdom.

**Fetch**   An easy-to-use file transfer program for the Macintosh. Sporting a simple graphic interface, it provides FTP file transfer (uploading and downloading) over the Internet.

**FTP (File Transfer Protocol)**   (n) A commonly used protocol for transferring files from one computer to another. (v) The act of transferring files (e.g., "I'm going to FTP that address book program from Info-Mac.").

**GIF (Graphic Interchange Format, pronounced "jiff")**   A file compression format developed by CompuServe for transferring graphics files to and from online services.

**Gopher**   A menu-driven system for searching online information resources.

**Gopherspace**   Another term used to describe the entire Gopher network that spans the Internet.

**Helper applications**   *See* External viewers.

**Home page**   The document that is displayed when you first open Mosaic. Also, commonly used to refer to the first document you come to in a collection of documents on a Web site.

**Hotlists**   Lists of frequently accessed Web location names and URLs.

**HTML (HyperText Markup Language)**   A system for tagging the various parts of a Web document that tells the browsing software how to display the document's text, links, graphics and attached media.

**HTML document**   Any document tagged in the HTML format. An HTML document that is accessible to the WWW is a Web document.

**HTTP servers**   (Hypertext Transport Protocol) A server computer that uses the communication protocol for Web document transfer.

**Hypermedia**   The hypertext concept extended to include linked multiple media such as graphics, movies and audio.

**Hypertext**   Documents that are cross-linked in such a way that the reader can explore non-linear information trails through them. (For example, clicking on a word might take you to a definition of that word or to another document related to it.)

**Inline images**   Graphics that are contained within a Web document page. With Mosaic, these graphics can either be loaded automatically when the page is accessed or loaded manually by clicking on an inline image icon.

**IP address (Internet Protocol)**   An IP address is a number assigned to any Internet-connected computer.

**JPEG (Joint Photographic Experts Group)**   An image compression format used to transfer color photographs and images over computer networks.

**JPEGView**   A program used for viewing graphics stored on the Net in the JPEG or GIF file formats. JPEGView is one of the default Helper Applications suggested for Mosaic.

**Links**   Synonymous with anchors, hotlinks and hyperlinks.

**MacTCP**   A program that allows a Macintosh to speak TCP/IP (Transmission Control Protocol/Internet Protocol), the communications protocol used on the Internet.

**MIME (Multi-purpose Internet Mail Extensions)**   A format originally developed for attaching sounds, images and other media files to electronic mail. MIME file types are also used in Mosaic.

**Mosaic**   A World Wide Web multimedia browser developed at the National Center for Supercomputing Applications at the University of Illinois, Urbana-Champaign. Mosaic is made available free of charge to the Internet community. Versions are available for the Mac, Windows and X Windows.

**MPEG (Moving Pictures Expert Group)**   MPEG is an international standard for video compression and desktop movie presentation. You need a special viewing application to run the MPEG "movies" on your computer.

**NCSA**   The National Center for Supercomputing Applications at the University of Illinois, Urbana-Champaign. Developers of Mosaic, NCSA Telnet and a number of other freeware applications.

**PPP connection (Point-to-Point Protocol)**   A type of Internet connection where a computer can use phone lines and a modem to connect to the Internet (without having to connect to a host). You must use PPP software in conjunction with MacTCP to establish the connection. PPP connections are rented from a local Internet service provider.

**QuickTime**   A digital video standard developed by Apple Computer. QuickTime is an extension file that goes in the System Folder. You need a special viewing application to run the QuickTime "movies" on your computer.

**Server**   A computer that offers various services (document viewing, file transfer, etc.) to other computers (called clients).

**SLIP connection (Serial Line Internet Protocol)**   A type of Internet connection where a computer can use phone lines and a modem to connect to the Internet (without having to connect to a host). You must use SLIP software in conjunction with MacTCP to establish the connection. SLIP connections are rented from a local Internet service provider.

**Tags**   Formatting codes used in HTML documents. These tags indicate how the parts of a document will appear when displayed by browsing software (such as Mosaic).

**Telnet**   An application that lets you log in to another system using the telnet protocol. NCSA Telnet is a freeware telnet program that can be used in conjunction with Mosaic.

**TIFF (Tagged Image File Format)**   A graphic file format developed by Aldus and Microsoft. Originally intended to be used with scanners, TIFF is now used as an image transfer format on computer networks. Mosaic supports the viewing of TIFF images.

**URL (Uniform Resource Locator)**   The addressing system used in the World Wide Web and a proposed addressing standard for the entire Internet. The URL contains information about the method of access, the server to be accessed and the path of any files to be accessed.

**WAIS (Wide Area Information Service)**   A Net-wide system for looking up information in databases and libraries.

**WAIS gateway**   A computer that is used to translate WAIS data so that it can be made available to an otherwise incompatible network or application. Since Mosaic cannot speak directly to WAIS, it must first go through a WAIS gateway.

**Web browser**   Software that allows a user to access and view HTML documents. Mosaic, Lynx and MacWeb are three examples of Web browsers.

**Web document**   An HTML document that is browsable on the WWW.

**Webmaster**   The person in charge of administrating a World Wide Web site.

**Web node**   Synonymous with Web site or Web server.

**Web page**   An HTML document that is accessible in the Web.

**Webspace**   Another term used to describe the "space" created by the WWW.

**Web spider**   Automated software that crawls through the links of the Web and sends back a list of all the links it's traversed.

**Web walking**   Using a Web browsing program to move through the documents available on the World Wide Web. The casual "browsing" nature of navigating the WWW has given rise to many slang terms that have to do with walking, strolling, crawling and jumping. As opposed to the more frantic metaphors found on the rest of the Internet (jacking in, data surfing, cyber run, etc.).

**World Wide Web**   The hypermedia document presentation system that can be accessed over the Internet using software called a browser. Mosaic is such a Web browser. Abbreviated as WWW.

**Zines**   *See* E-zines.

# BIBLIOGRAPHY

## Books

Aboba, Bernard. *The Online User's Encyclopedia*. New York, NY: Addison-Wesley, 1994.

Basch, Reva. *Secrets of the Super Searchers*. Wilton, CT: Eight Bit Books, 1993.

Bayers, Albert F. III, Peter Rutten, and Kelly Maloni. *Net Guide*. New York, NY: Random House, 1994.

Fraase, Michael. *The Mac Internet Tour Guide*. Chapel Hill, NC: Ventana Press, 1993.

Hahn, Harley, and Rick Stout. *The Internet Complete Reference*. Berkeley, CA: Osborne McGraw-Hill, 1994.

———. *The Internet Yellow Pages*. Berkeley, CA: Osborne McGraw-Hill, 1994.

Kirby, Doug, Mike Wilkins, and Ken Smith. *New Roadside America*. New York, NY: Simon & Schuster, 1992.

Krol, Ed. *The Whole Internet User's Guide and Catalog*. Second edition. Sebastopol, CA: O'Reilly & Associates, 1994.

Lambert, S., and W. Howe. *Internet Basics*. New York, NY: Random House, 1994.

McLuhan, Marshall. *Understanding Media: The Extensions of Man*. New York: McGraw-Hill, 1965.

Rheingold, Howard. *The Virtual Community: Homesteading on the Electronic Frontier*. New York, NY: Addison-Wesley, 1993.

Stephenson, Neil. *Snow Crash*. New York, NY: Bantam, 1992.

Williams, Robin. *Jargon: An Informal Dictionary of Computer Terms*. Berkeley, CA: Peachpit Press, 1993.

## Periodicals

*3W—The World Wide Web Newsletter*, 461 West 49th St., Suite 338, New York, NY 10019. Bi-monthly.

*Wired*, P.O. Box 191826, San Francisco, CA 94119-9866. Monthly.

# INDEX

# COLOPHON

This book was developed on a Macintosh Quadra 650. All pages were produced in Aldus PageMaker 5.0. Some graphics were produced or edited in Adobe Photoshop 2.5.1 and Adobe Illustrator 5.0. Chapter titles are set in Anna. Chapter numbers are set in Futura Condensed Bold. The body text is Palatino with Futura Heavy subheads. Tables and sidebars are set in Futura. The title of the book (on the cover and title pages) is set in Michelangelo.

# MACINTOSH
## MAC BOOKS—MAGIC & MASTERY

### Explore Cyberspace!

*The Mac Internet Tour Guide*
$27.95, 300 pages, illustrated
ISBN: 1-56604-062-0

Mac users can now navigate the Internet the easy way: by pointing and clicking, dragging and dropping. In easy-to-read, entertaining prose, Internet expert Michael Fraase leads you through installing and using the software enclosed in the book to send and receive email, transfer files, search the Internet's vast resources and more! BONUS: Free trial access and two free electronic updates.

### Handy 3-in-1 Guide!

*Mac, Word & Excel Desktop Companion, Second Edition*
$24.95, 308 pages, illustrated
ISBN: 1-56604-130-9

Why clutter your desk with three guides? This money saver gets you up and running with Apple's System 7.1 software and the latest versions of Microsoft Word and Excel for the Mac. A complete overview, examples of each program's commands, tools and features and step-by-step tutorials guide you easily along the learning curve for maximum Macintosh productivity!

### Software $avings!

*The Mac Shareware 500, Second Edition*
$34.95, 459 pages, illustrated
ISBN: 1-56604-076-0

A fantastic reference for any designer or desktop publisher interested in saving money by using the vast resources shareware offers. This book is a complete guide to the thousands of fonts, graphics, clip-art files and utilities are available for downloading via dozens of online services. To get you started, this book includes two disks of shareware.

MACINTOSH
Mac Macintosh
Mac Mac Mac
Mac Mac

### Join 1,000,000 Friends Online!

*The Official America Online Membership Kit & Tour Guide, Second Edition*
$27.95, 406 pages, illustrated
ISBN: 1-56604-127-9

This book takes Mac users on a lively romp through the friendly AOL cyberscape. Bestselling author Tom Lichty, a.k.a. MajorTom, shows you how to make friends and find your way around, and save time and money online. Complete with software to get you started. BONUS: 10 free hours of online time for new and current members and a free month's membership.

### Mac Magic!

*Voodoo Mac, Second Edition*
$24.95, 459 pages, illustrated
ISBN: 1-56604-177-5

Whether you're a power user looking for new shortcuts or a beginner trying to make sense of it all, *Voodoo Mac* has something for everyone! Author Kay Nelson has compiled hundreds of invaluable tips, tricks, hints and shortcuts that simplify your Macintosh tasks and save time, including disk and drive magic, font and printing tips, alias alchemy and more!

### Now for System 7.5!

*The System 7.5 Book, Third Edition*
$24.95, 459 pages, illustrated
ISBN: 1-56604-129-5

The all-time bestselling *System 7 Book*, now revised, updated and re-titled! With over 120,000 copies in print, *The System 7.5 Book* is the industry's recognized standard and the last word on the Macintosh and PowerMac operating systems. A complete overview of AppleHelp, AOCE, e-mail, fax, PC Exchange, MacTCP, QuickTime and more!

# DESIGN AND CONQUER!

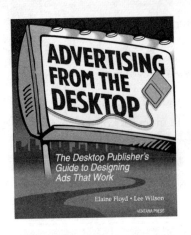

## Advertising From the Desktop

$24.95
427 pages, illustrated
ISBN: 1-56604-064-7

*Advertising From the Desktop* offers unmatched design advice and helpful how-to instructions for creating persuasive ads. With tips on how to choose fonts, select illustrations, apply special effects and more, this book is an idea-packed resource for improving the looks and effects of your ads.

## The Presentation Design Book, Second Edition

$24.95
320 pages, illustrated
ISBN: 1-56604-014-0

*The Presentation Design Book* is filled with thoughtful advice and instructive examples for creating business presentation visuals, including charts, overheads, type, etc., that help you communicate and persuade. The *Second Edition* adds advice on the use of multimedia. For use with any software or hardware.

## The Gray Book, Second Edition

$24.95

262 pages, illustrated

ISBN: 1-56604-073-6

This "idea gallery" for desktop publishers offers a lavish variety of the most interesting black, white and gray graphic effects that can be achieved with laser printers, scanners and high-resolution output devices. The *Second Edition* features new illustrations, synopses and steps, added tips and an updated appendix.

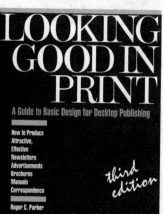

## Looking Good in Print, Third Edition

$24.95

412 pages, illustrated

ISBN: 1-56604-047-7

For use with any software or hardware, this desktop design bible has become the standard among novice and experienced desktop publishers alike. With over 200,000 copies in print, *Looking Good in Print* is even better, with new sections on photography and scanning.

## Newsletters From the Desktop, Second Edition

$24.95

306 pages, illustrated

ISBN: 1-56604-133-3

Now the millions of desktop publishers who produce newsletters can learn how to improve the design of their publications. Filled with helpful design tips and illustrations.

# Can't wait? Call toll-free: 800/743-5369 (U.S. only)

# INTERNET. HERE. NOW.

For Windows or Macintosh

## Internet
### Membership Kit™

**$200 Value!**
- Free access offer — one month plus 6 hours free from CERFnet!
- Easy E-mail software
- Graphical Search
- File transfer and compression software
- Two bestselling guide books
- Internet Visitors Center

**Everything You Need to Cruise the Information Superhighway**

## 1-800-209-3342

Ventana Media announces the **INTERNET MEMBERSHIP KIT**, your easy-access on-ramp to the information superhighway. Both **MACINTOSH** and **WINDOWS** versions put you in control of a sleek **GRAPHICAL INTERFACE**—skip frustrating command-line gibberish and take advantage of the Internet's vast information resources with point-and-click convenience. The Kit includes two national bestsellers, *The Internet Tour Guide* and *The Internet Yellow Pages*, plus a one-month **FREE MEMBERSHIP** with CERFnet and **SIX FREE HOURS** online. Also included are step-by-step instructions for using **MOSAIC**, one of the most powerful tools available to information surfers, as well as all the software you'll need to get up and running in no time! Suggested retail price $69.95.

| | Quantity | Price | | Total |
|---|---|---|---|---|
| *The Mac Internet Tour Guide* | _____ x | $27.95 | = | $ _____ |
| *Mac, Word & Excel Desktop Companion, 2nd Edition* | _____ x | $24.95 | = | $ _____ |
| *The Mac Shareware 500, 2nd Edition* | _____ x | $34.95 | = | $ _____ |
| *The Official America Online Membership Kit & Tour Guide for Macintosh, 2nd Edition* | _____ x | $27.95 | = | $ _____ |
| *Voodoo Mac, Second Edition* | _____ x | $24.95 | = | $ _____ |
| *The System 7.5 Book, 3rd Edition* | _____ x | $24.95 | = | $ _____ |
| *Advertising From the Desktop* | _____ x | $24.95 | = | $ _____ |
| *The Presentation Design Book, 2nd Edition* | _____ x | $24.95 | = | $ _____ |
| *The Gray Book, 2nd Edition* | _____ x | $24.95 | = | $ _____ |
| *Looking Good in Print, 3rd Edition* | _____ x | $24.95 | = | $ _____ |
| *Newsletters From the Desktop, 2nd Edition* | _____ x | $24.95 | = | $ _____ |
| *Internet Membership Kit, Macintosh Version* | _____ x | $69.95 | = | $ _____ |
| *Internet Membership Kit, Windows Version* | _____ x | $69.95 | = | $ _____ |
| | | Subtotal | = | $ _____ |

SHIPPING:

For all regular orders, please <u>add</u> $4.50/first book, $1.35/each additional.    = $ _____
For Internet Membership Kit orders, <u>add</u> $6.50/first kit, $2.00/each additional.    = $ _____
For "two-day air" on books, <u>add</u> $8.25/first book, $2.25/each additional.    = $ _____
For "two-day air" on the IMK, <u>add</u> $10.50/first kit, $4.00/each additional.    = $ _____
For orders to Canada, <u>add</u> $6.50/book.    = $ _____
For orders sent C.O.D., <u>add</u> $4.50 to your shipping rate.    = $ _____
North Carolina residents must <u>add</u> 6% sales tax.    = $ _____
TOTAL = $ _____

Name _____ Company _____

Address (No PO Box) _____

City _____ State _____ Zip _____

Daytime Telephone _____

___ Payment enclosed ___ VISA ___ MC Acc't # _____ Expiration Date ____

Signature _____

Mail or fax to: Ventana Press, PO Box 2468, Chapel Hill, NC 27515  ☎ 919/942-0220 Fax 919/942-1140